Living Islam with Purpose

Nurturing Faith and Balance in a Modern World

Aisha Othman, Esquire

Dedication

In the Name of Allah, the Most Gracious, the Most Merciful

This book is dedicated

To those on a journey toward a life of meaning, rooted in faith and guided by purpose.

To my family, whose support and love inspire me to strive for a life aligned with Islamic values every day.

To the teachers and scholars, past and present, who illuminate the path of knowledge, wisdom, and resilience through their words and actions.

And to every Muslim community working to embody compassion, justice, and unity — may this book be a source of benefit and a small contribution to our collective journey toward Allah.

May Allah accept this effort and grant us all steadfastness in our purpose, sincerity in our actions, and peace in our hearts. Aameen.

-Aisha Othman

First edition, 2024

Contents

Preface

In the Name of Allah, the Most Merciful, the Most Compassionate.

All Praise is for Allah, the Lord of the Worlds. We praise Him, seek His forgiveness, and ask for His protection from the accursed Satan. Whomsoever He guides, none can misguide, and whomsoever He allows to be misguided, none can guide.

I bear witness that there is no deity worthy of worship except Allah, alone without any partners. I bear witness that Muhammad is His servant and His Messenger. May Allah's blessings and peace be upon our liege-lord Muhammad, the seal of the prophets, sent to perfect noble character, the leader of the God-fearing, and upon his family, his Companions, and all those who follow them in righteousness until the Day of Judgment.

I ask Allah to purify my intentions, to make this work sincerely for His sake, and to grant me and my family success in this life and the next. He is my sufficiency, and how perfect a Benefactor is He. May Allah bless every reader of this book with increased blessings and a deeper love for Allah and His Messenger (peace and blessings be upon him) both in this world and the Hereafter.

All praise is due to Allah, Lord of the Worlds. If this work is successful, it is due to Allah's generosity; if there are mistakes, they are from my shortcomings. I ask Allah to guide and protect me and my family, for He supports those who rely on Him. I seek Allah's forgiveness for my shortcomings and pray for His blessings of well-being and success in this world and the next.

The journey to live with purpose, grounded in Islamic values, is a lifelong endeavor that transcends daily routines, cultural expectations, and even personal ambitions. Islam, with its holistic teachings and timeless guidance, offers believers a way to navigate life with clarity, resilience, and a sense of direction. This book explores what it means to live Islam with purpose, examining both the personal spiritual journey and the communal responsibilities that shape a meaningful life.

In today's world, Muslims face unique challenges and opportunities. With the pressures of secularism, the pace of modern life, and a constant influx of information, it is easy to become distracted or even disconnected from the deeper meanings and goals that Islam sets before us. This book seeks to address these concerns by delving into topics that impact every Muslim's journey: nurturing an individual connection with Allah, seeking beneficial knowledge, trusting in His wisdom, building supportive communities, and finding a balance between personal and communal obligations.

The insights within these pages draw from classical Islamic teachings, the lives of the Prophet Muhammad (peace and blessings be upon him) and his companions, and the writings of scholars like Imam al-Haddad, Ibn Ata'illah, and Imam Ghazali. Their wisdom offers valuable lessons for contemporary Muslims, reminding us that while the world may change, the principles of purpose, devotion, and community are enduring.

This book is intended for anyone seeking to deepen their understanding of how to live Islam authentically in both private and public spheres. It is for those striving to create lives filled with meaning, resilience, and a commitment to Allah and His creation. I hope that each chapter provides not only knowledge but also inspiration and practical guidance for readers to incorporate purpose into their everyday lives.

May Allah accept this humble effort and make it a source of benefit for those who read it. May it serve as a reminder that every action, if done with sincere intention, can bring us closer to Allah and contribute to a life of true purpose. Aameen.

Aisha Othman
November 2024 / Jumada al-Awwal 1446
California, USA
Dar An-Noor for Islamic Education and Arts
www.darannoor.com

Introduction: The Quest for Purpose in Islam

I slam provides a profound and comprehensive understanding of purpose, offering believers a clear direction that encompasses both personal growth and communal responsibility. This chapter examines the Islamic perspective on purpose, exploring its roots in worship and servitude, the insights of classical scholars, and its relevance in the modern world. By understanding purpose from an Islamic viewpoint, Muslims can anchor their lives in spirituality, gain clarity in their daily actions, and cultivate a life that is meaningful and fulfilling.

Introduction to Purpose: Worship and Servitude

The concept of purpose in Islam is rooted in worship (*ibadah*) and servitude (*ubudiyyah*) to Allah. Islam teaches that humans are created with a distinct objective: to recognize, worship, and serve Allah, aligning every aspect of their lives with His guidance. The Quran captures this in a powerful ayah: "And I did not create the jinn and mankind except to worship Me" (Quran, Adh-Dhariyat 51:56). This statement establishes worship as the primary purpose of existence, one that encompasses all facets of a believer's life.

Worship in Islam is not confined to rituals like prayer (Salah), fasting, charity, or Hajj. Instead, it extends to all actions done with sincerity for Allah's sake, transforming mundane tasks into meaningful acts of devotion. The Prophet Muhammad (peace and blessings be upon him) taught, "The best of deeds are those done consistently, even if they are small." (Sahih Bukhari, Sahih Muslim). In this way, every action—whether working, eating, or engaging in family life—can become an expression of worship if carried out with the intention of fulfilling one's duty to Allah.

Servitude (*ubudiyyah*) complements worship, emphasizing a life of submission, obedience, and humility before Allah. *Ubudiyyah* is the continuous effort to align one's intentions, actions, and desires with the divine will. It reminds believers that they are servants of Allah, responsible for living in accordance with His guidance. This servitude is not restrictive; rather, it liberates the individual from the chains of ego, materialism, and worldly distractions, fostering a life of purpose that transcends the transient nature of the world.

Together, worship and servitude create a holistic understanding of purpose in Islam, guiding believers to lead lives of devotion, selflessness, and integrity. This purpose is not only about individual fulfillment but also about contributing to the well-being of the community, embodying values of compassion, justice, and humility.

The Influence of Islamic Scholars on Purpose

Islamic scholarship has long explored the concept of purpose, with many classical scholars offering profound insights on how to live a life aligned with Allah's guidance. Scholars like Imam al-Haddad, Ibn Ata'illah, and Imam Ghazali are known for their deep reflections on purpose, spirituality, and self-discipline. Their works continue to guide Muslims toward meaningful living, providing timeless wisdom that addresses both personal and communal aspects of life.

Imam al-Haddad and the Purification of the Heart: Imam al-Haddad, a Yemeni scholar and Sufi master, emphasized that true purpose begins with the purification of the heart. In his famous work, *The Book of Assistance*, he teaches that the heart is the seat of intention and must be purified of negative qualities, such as pride, envy, and attachment to worldly desires, to attain a sincere connection with Allah. He asserts that a heart filled with sincere devotion can turn every action into a form of worship, thereby enabling a life of purpose and inner peace. His teachings highlight the importance of sincerity (*ikhlas*) and intention (*niyyah*) in all actions. He encourages Muslims to strive for purity of heart, as this is the foundation of a purposeful life. By removing distractions and focusing on pleasing Allah, a believer can achieve a state of spiritual tranquility and alignment with divine guidance.

Ibn Ata'illah and Trust in Divine Wisdom: Ibn Ata'illah, an Egyptian scholar and Sufi master, explores purpose through the lens of *tawakkul* (trust in Allah) and *ridha* (contentment with Allah's decree). In his *Kitab al-Hikam* (Book of Wisdom), he writes, "If you are not content with what Allah has allotted for you, how can you expect the sweetness of faith?" For Ibn Ata'illah, purpose is deeply tied to understanding that Allah's wisdom governs all affairs. He encourages believers to find peace in the knowledge that Allah's plan is always for the best, even if it is beyond human comprehension. He teaches that hardships and challenges are not obstacles to purpose but are, in fact, integral to it. He explains that trials bring believers closer to Allah, helping them develop patience, humility, and resilience. By placing trust in Allah and accepting His decree, a person can navigate life's difficulties with a sense of purpose and inner strength, seeing each moment as an opportunity for spiritual growth.

Imam Ghazali and the Pursuit of Knowledge: Imam Ghazali, one of Islam's most influential thinkers, addresses the concept of purpose extensively in *Ihya' Ulum al-Din* (The Revival of the Religious Sciences). He emphasizes that the human soul's ultimate purpose is to attain knowledge of Allah and draw closer to Him. He describes the soul's journey as continuous learning, spiritual refinement, and self-purification. Knowledge, according to Imam Ghazali, illuminates the path to Allah, allowing a person to see beyond the illusions of the world and recognize the reality of divine wisdom. He categorizes knowledge into two types: the outward knowledge of Islamic law (*fiqh*) and the inward knowledge of spirituality (*tasawwuf*). Both types are essential for a purposeful life, as they provide a framework for ethical conduct and inner transformation. He warns against seeking knowledge for personal gain, stating that knowledge should be pursued solely for the sake of Allah, as this leads to true fulfillment and spiritual liberation.

Each of these scholars contributes unique insights on purpose, emphasizing the need for sincerity, trust, knowledge, and inner purification. Their teachings offer a roadmap for living Islam as a complete way of life, guiding believers to navigate both spiritual and worldly matters with wisdom, patience, and devotion.

Why Purpose Matters Today

The quest for purpose has become increasingly significant in the modern world, where secularism, materialism, and individualism often dominate. Many people struggle with emptiness despite achieving worldly success or fulfilling social expectations. Islam offers a solution to this crisis of meaning, providing a purpose rooted in spiritual and ethical values, transcending the temporary pleasures of the world.

Purpose as a Source of Stability and Resilience:
- A life of purpose provides stability, helping individuals remain grounded amid life's challenges and uncertainties. When people's purpose is based on their relationship with Allah, they gain resilience in the face of hardships. This sense of purpose strengthens them, enabling them to handle setbacks with patience and faith.

- Islam teaches that true success lies in fulfilling one's duty to Allah and striving for the Hereafter instead of chasing fleeting worldly gains. This perspective liberates individuals from the pressures of societal expectations, allowing them to lead lives of contentment, gratitude, and inner peace.

Purpose in a Secular World:
- In secular societies, religion may be perceived as irrelevant or outdated. However, Islam's concept of purpose offers a timeless solution, guiding believers to lead meaningful and morally grounded lives. This purpose is not limited to personal goals but extends to social responsibility, encouraging Muslims to contribute to the well-being of others and uphold justice, compassion, and integrity.

- By embracing this purpose, Muslims can live as role models of ethical conduct, kindness, and resilience. They can demonstrate that a life centered on spirituality and service is fulfilling and impactful, even in a world that often values material success over moral character.

Purpose as a Path to Personal and Communal Well-Being:
- Purpose not only enhances individual spirituality but also strengthens the community. A person who lives with purpose strives to benefit others, fulfill their obligations, and contribute to a just society. This communal aspect of purpose reflects Islam's emphasis on interconnectedness, where each person's actions have a ripple effect on the wider community.

- When individuals and communities align their lives with Islamic values, they create environments that promote peace, cooperation, and compassion. This fosters a sense of belonging, unity, and shared responsibility, transforming society into one that reflects the principles of mercy, kindness, and justice.

In a world where many are searching for meaning, Islam's concept of purpose serves as a guiding light, offering clarity, strength, and hope. By aligning their lives with this purpose, Muslims can cultivate a sense of fulfillment that is not dependent on external achievements but is rooted in faith and devotion to Allah.

Purpose in Daily Life

Islam encourages believers to integrate purpose into every action, beginning with a sincere intention (*niyyah*). The Prophet Muhammad (peace and blessings be upon him) said, "Actions are judged by intentions, and every person will get what they intended." (Sahih Bukhari). This hadith highlights the transformative power of intention, turning even ordinary tasks into acts of worship when done for Allah's sake. A life of purpose, therefore, is one where every action—whether big or small—is infused with meaning and directed toward Allah.

Purposeful Living Through Daily Actions:

- **Work and Livelihood**: Islam considers earning a lawful income and supporting one's family as acts of worship. When a person works with the intention of fulfilling their responsibilities and pleasing Allah, their work becomes a means of spiritual fulfillment. This perspective transforms work from a mere pursuit of wealth into a purposeful endeavor that contributes to the welfare of oneself and others.

- **Family and Relationships**: Islam places great importance on maintaining healthy relationships with family, friends, and the community. By approaching relationships with compassion, patience, and forgiveness, a believer reflects the values of mercy and kindness that Allah commands. Purposeful interactions strengthen bonds and foster a sense of love, care, and mutual respect.

- **Charity and Service**: The Quran encourages charity, stating, "The example of those who spend their wealth in the way of Allah is like a seed that sprouts seven ears; in every ear is a hundred seeds." (Quran, Al-Baqarah 2:261). Giving charity, supporting the needy, and contributing to communal well-being are expressions of one's purpose as a steward of Allah's blessings. These acts of generosity reflect a commitment to serving humanity and fulfilling one's responsibility as a member of the community.

Purpose in Facing Challenges:

- **Patience and Resilience**: Life's challenges test a believer's purpose, pushing them to seek strength through patience (*sabr*) and reliance on Allah. Trials are not merely obstacles but opportunities for growth, refinement, and a deeper connection with Allah. By facing difficulties with faith and resilience, a person strengthens their trust in Allah and fortifies their sense of purpose.

- **Seeking Allah's Help**: Islam teaches that no hardship is too great when one turns to Allah for guidance and support. Through prayer and supplication, a believer finds peace and strength, knowing that Allah is always present and attentive. This reliance on Allah during difficult times reinforces the purpose of life as a journey of faith, patience, and submission.

Preview of Key Themes

This book will delve deeper into the quest for purpose in Islam, exploring several key themes that provide a comprehensive framework for living Islam in every aspect of life:

- **Individual Spiritual Practices**: The following chapters will discuss practices like prayer (Salah), supplication, and self-reflection, which foster a personal relationship with Allah. These practices are essential for nurturing a heart that is devoted, sincere, and focused on fulfilling its purpose.

- **Role of Community**: Islam places great importance on community, with mosques and Islamic organizations serving as centers of spiritual growth and social support. This book will explore how these institutions can contribute to or hinder one's sense of purpose, highlighting the importance of inclusivity, compassion, and leadership in nurturing a vibrant community.

- **Personal and Organizational Failures**: Purpose is not about perfection but about continuous effort, learning, and growth. This book will examine both individual and organizational challenges, providing lessons on resilience, forgiveness, and the journey of self-improvement.

- **Enduring Value of Islamic Scholarship**: The teachings of scholars like Imam al-Haddad, Ibn Ata'illah, and Imam Ghazali will serve as guiding principles throughout this book. Their wisdom continues to inspire Muslims to seek knowledge, purify their hearts, and trust in Allah's wisdom, enabling them to live lives of purpose and integrity.

Through these themes, this book will offer insights into integrating purpose into daily life, fostering personal and communal well-being, and drawing closer to Allah. The following chapters provide a roadmap for embracing purpose as an ongoing journey, empowering readers to lead meaningful lives that reflect the beauty and depth of Islamic teachings.

CHAPTER ONE

Living Islam: An Individual Journey

L iving Islam is a deeply personal journey that requires a continuous, intentional effort to connect with Allah, seek beneficial knowledge, place unwavering trust in His wisdom, and engage in self-accountability. These foundational aspects serve as pillars that support a meaningful life aligned with Islamic principles, guiding believers toward a purposeful existence. This chapter explores these elements in depth, offering practical insights into how Muslims can deepen their individual relationship with Allah and strive for continuous self-improvement in every aspect of life.

1.1 Connecting to Allah: Daily Practices, Intentions, and Purity of Heart

A central aspect of living Islam is cultivating a constant connection with Allah. This relationship is nurtured through intentional daily acts of worship, setting sincere intentions, and maintaining a pure heart that is focused on pleasing Allah. The Quran reminds believers, "And establish prayer for My remembrance" (Quran, Ta-Ha 20:14), emphasizing the importance of regular, mindful worship to keep one's heart and mind connected to Allah.

Daily Practices to Connect with Allah:

- **Prayer (Salah)**: The five daily prayers are the cornerstone of a Muslim's connection with Allah. Each prayer offers a structured moment to pause, disconnect from worldly distractions, and focus entirely on Allah. The Prophet (peace and blessings be upon him) described prayer as "the coolness of my eyes" (Sunan an-Nasa'i, 3939; Musnad Ahmad, 13720), highlighting its role as a source of solace and spiritual rejuvenation. Through each bow and prostration, believers express humility, devotion, and gratitude, reinforcing their bond with Allah and reaffirming their purpose.

- **Supplication (Du'a)**: Du'a is a direct form of communication with Allah, allowing believers to express their hopes, fears, and gratitude. Unlike formal prayer, Du'a can be made at any time and in any language, making it a highly personal and intimate act of worship. The Prophet Muhammad (peace and blessings be upon him) called Du'a "the essence of worship" (Sunan At-Tirmidhi, 3371; Musnad Ahmad, 17837), underscoring its importance in a Muslim's daily life. By regularly turning to Allah in Du'a, a believer strengthens their relationship with Him, knowing that He listens and responds to every sincere call.

- **Remembrance (Dhikr)**: Dhikr, or the act of remembering Allah, keeps a believer's heart and mind engaged with the Creator throughout the day. Simple phrases like "SubhanAllah" (Glory be to Allah), "Alhamdulillah" (All praise is due to Allah), and "Allahu Akbar" (Allah is Greater) serve as constant reminders of Allah's presence and blessings. Dhikr helps believers maintain a spiritual focus, cultivating inner peace and reinforcing their purpose in life as servants of Allah.

Setting Intentions (Niyyah):

The concept of *niyyah*, or intention, is a core principle in Islam that emphasizes the importance of sincerity in every action. The Prophet Muhammad (peace and blessings be upon him) said, "Actions are judged by intentions, and every person will get what they intended." (Sahih Bukhari; Sahih Muslim). This hadith highlights how the intention behind an action determines its value in the eyes of Allah. When a Muslim sets a sincere intention, even ordinary activities like working, eating, or spending time with family become acts of worship if done with the purpose of fulfilling one's duties as a Muslim.

- Intentions act as a compass that directs a believer's actions toward Allah, helping them stay mindful of their spiritual goals. By regularly renewing their intentions, Muslims can guard against ego-driven motives, pride, or the desire for recognition, ensuring that their actions remain solely for Allah's pleasure. This sincerity of intention transforms every aspect of life into a meaningful journey of devotion and self-purification.

Purity of Heart:

Maintaining a pure heart is essential to connecting deeply with Allah. Imam al-Ghazali, a prominent Islamic scholar, teaches that a pure heart is one free from envy, pride, greed, and other negative traits that cloud a person's ability to worship Allah sincerely. The Prophet Muhammad (peace and blessings be upon him) said, "Truly, in the body, there is a morsel of flesh which, if it is sound, all the body is sound; and if it is corrupt, all the body is corrupt. Truly, it is the heart." (Sahih Bukhari; Sahih Muslim). This highlights the significance of the heart as the center of spiritual well-being and moral integrity.

- Purifying the heart requires ongoing self-reflection, repentance, and a conscious effort to replace negative traits with positive virtues. A purified heart enables believers to approach Allah with humility, compassion, and sincerity, allowing them to experience inner peace and satisfaction. This inner purity is a cornerstone of purpose-driven living, as it fosters a life aligned with Allah's guidance and grounded in genuine devotion.

1.2 Seeking Knowledge: The Importance of Pursuing Islamic Knowledge

Islam places great emphasis on the pursuit of knowledge, viewing it as an essential means of understanding Allah's guidance and achieving spiritual growth. Seeking knowledge is an act of worship that not only deepens a believer's understanding of their faith but also enables them to fulfill their purpose with greater clarity and intention. Imam al-Ghazali, in his monumental work *Ihya' Ulum al-Din* (The Revival of the Religious Sciences), emphasizes the transformative power of knowledge in guiding the soul toward Allah.

The Role of Knowledge in Spiritual Growth:

- **Understanding Divine Guidance**: Knowledge is the key to understanding Allah's commandments, ethical principles, and values. By studying the Quran, Hadith, and classical Islamic teachings, believers understand what is permissible, forbidden, and praiseworthy. This understanding empowers Muslims to make choices that align with

divine guidance, leading them closer to Allah and helping them fulfill
their purpose.

- **Enhancing Acts of Worship**: Knowledge enriches a believer's acts of
worship, transforming them into meaningful, mindful practices. For
instance, understanding the meanings of the verses recited in prayer
allows a person to connect more deeply with Allah during Salah.
Similarly, knowledge of the Prophet Muhammad's (peace and blessings
be upon him) teachings on humility, gratitude, and patience enhances a
believer's character and brings depth to their worship.

- **Imam al-Ghazali's Perspective on Knowledge**: Imam al-Ghazali
categorizes knowledge into outward knowledge, such as Islamic
jurisprudence (*fiqh*), and inward knowledge, which pertains to spiritual
purification. While outward knowledge provides a framework for
lawful living, inward knowledge refines the soul, fostering qualities
like humility, sincerity, and reliance on Allah. Together, these types of
knowledge equip a believer to live a life of purpose that is pleasing to
Allah.

Practical Steps in Seeking Knowledge:

- **Starting with the Essentials**: Every Muslim should begin their
journey of knowledge by understanding the basics of Islamic beliefs,
practices, and ethics. These fundamentals form a solid foundation upon
which deeper spiritual knowledge can be built.

- **Delving into Quranic and Hadith Studies**: As one's knowledge
grows, studying the Quran and Hadith provides deeper insights into
Islam's core teachings. Reading Tafsir (exegesis of the Quran) and
Hadith commentaries offers context, clarifies meanings, and provides
guidance on living in accordance with Allah's commands.

- **Approaching Learning with Humility**: Imam al-Ghazali warns
against seeking knowledge for personal gain or social status. Knowledge
in Islam is a means of drawing closer to Allah, not a tool for
self-promotion or superiority. Approaching learning with humility
ensures that knowledge becomes a path to spiritual growth rather than
a source of pride or arrogance.

The Lifelong Pursuit of Knowledge:

Seeking knowledge is a lifelong endeavor in Islam, as there is always more to learn and understand. This continuous pursuit keeps a believer's mind and heart engaged, renewing their faith and strengthening their connection to Allah. By seeking beneficial knowledge at every stage of life, Muslims can enrich their understanding of faith, cultivate inner peace, and draw closer to fulfilling their purpose.

1.3 Relying on Allah (Tawakkul): Trust in Allah's Plans

Tawakkul, or reliance on Allah, is a fundamental aspect of a Muslim's faith, teaching believers to place their trust in Allah's wisdom and mercy in all circumstances. Trusting in Allah does not mean abandoning one's responsibilities; rather, it is about making sincere efforts and leaving the results in Allah's hands, accepting that His plan is always for the best. Ibn Ata'illah, a renowned scholar and Sufi master, explores this concept in his *Kitab al-Hikam* (Book of Wisdom), offering profound insights into the nature of divine reliance.

The Meaning of Tawakkul:

Tawakkul involves an active engagement with life, where a believer takes the necessary steps to fulfill their duties while remaining content with Allah's decree. Ibn Ata'illah describes tawakkul as a state of trust that brings peace and acceptance, even in the face of uncertainty. He states, "If you are not content with what Allah has allotted for you, how can you expect the sweetness of faith?" This emphasizes that true reliance on Allah requires both trust and contentment.

Trusting Allah Amid Life's Trials:

- **Embracing Allah's Wisdom in Hardships**: Life's challenges are often beyond human control, and *Tawakkul* teaches that every hardship is an opportunity to draw closer to Allah. The Prophet Muhammad (peace and blessings be upon him) said, "How wonderful is the affair of the believer, for his affairs are all good. If something good happens to him, he is thankful, and that is good for him. If something harmful happens to him, he is patient, and that is good for him." (Muslim). This statement illustrates how tawakkul transforms challenges into valuable lessons of gratitude and patience.

* **Ibn Ata'illah on Divine Wisdom**: Ibn Ata'illah's writings emphasize that both ease and hardship are manifestations of Allah's mercy. He teaches that what may seem like a setback is, in fact, an opportunity for spiritual growth and a test of faith. Through trials, Allah draws believers closer to Him, helping them develop patience, resilience, and reliance on His divine wisdom.

Cultivating Tawakkul in Daily Life:

* **Reflecting on Allah's Attributes**: By contemplating Allah's attributes, such as Al-Rahman (the Most Merciful) and Al-Hakim (the Most Wise), believers can strengthen their trust in His plan. This reflection reinforces the understanding that Allah's knowledge is perfect and that every event in life, whether pleasant or difficult, is part of His divine wisdom.

* **Practicing Patience and Prayer**: *Tawakkul* is closely linked to patience (*Sabr*) and prayer. When faced with difficulties, a believer can turn to Allah in prayer, seeking His help and guidance. This act of devotion reinforces the believer's reliance on Allah and provides comfort and reassurance during times of hardship.

The Benefits of Tawakkul:

Tawakkul brings peace, reduces worry, and nurtures a sense of gratitude. By placing trust in Allah, believers are freed from the constant anxiety of trying to control every aspect of their lives. This trust empowers them to face life's challenges with resilience and confidence, knowing that Allah's plan is always in their best interest.

1.4 Personal Accountability: Examining Oneself and Rectifying Faults

Personal accountability, or *Muhasabah*, is a practice that encourages individuals to regularly assess their actions, intentions, and moral character. Self-accountability is essential for spiritual growth, as it enables believers to recognize their weaknesses, seek forgiveness, and strive for self-improvement. Imam al-Ghazali emphasizes that without regular self-reflection, a person's spiritual journey remains stagnant, as they cannot identify and correct the flaws that hinder their relationship with Allah.

The Importance of Self-Reflection:

- **A Path to Spiritual Refinement**: Self-reflection allows individuals to become aware of traits like pride, envy, anger, or impatience that may interfere with their spiritual progress. By acknowledging these flaws, a believer takes the first step toward personal refinement, striving to cultivate virtues that bring them closer to Allah.

- **Imam al-Ghazali's Guidance on Self-Accountability**: Ghazali advises that *Muhasabah* should be a daily practice. He encourages believers to set aside time each day to reflect on their words, actions, and intentions, asking questions like, "Did I fulfill my duties to Allah and others today?" This habit fosters a conscientious attitude, keeping a person focused on their purpose and committed to continuous improvement.

Practical Steps in Personal Accountability:

- **Daily Self-Review**: At the end of each day, a Muslim can take a few moments to reflect on their behavior, considering how well they uphold Islamic values in their interactions, thoughts, and deeds. This daily practice encourages mindfulness and helps believers identify areas for growth.

- **Seeking Forgiveness**: Recognizing one's faults is a precursor to seeking Allah's forgiveness. Through sincere repentance (*Tawbah*), believers can purify their hearts and renew their intention to follow the path of righteousness.

- **Setting Goals for Improvement**: Accountability is most effective when accompanied by actionable goals. By setting realistic goals for self-improvement, such as increasing patience or avoiding negative speech, a believer can make steady progress toward spiritual refinement.

Emulating the Prophet's Example:

The Prophet Muhammad (peace and blessings be upon him) exemplified humility and self-accountability. Though he was sinless, he frequently sought forgiveness from Allah, setting an example of humility and continuous self-reflection. His life serves as a reminder that every believer, regardless of their level of piety, has room for growth and a need for regular self-examination.

In conclusion, living Islam as an individual journey requires intentional worship, the pursuit of beneficial knowledge, unwavering trust in Allah, and regular self-accountability. Each of these practices is essential for cultivating a deep, meaningful relationship with Allah and living a life of purpose. By nurturing these qualities, Muslims can achieve inner peace, resilience, and fulfillment, embodying the beauty and depth of Islamic teachings in every aspect of life. This journey, though challenging, is a path to true contentment, guiding believers toward the ultimate goal of closeness to Allah and eternal success.

CHAPTER TWO

Living Islam: Integrating Worship and Ethics

L iving Islam is more than performing acts of worship—it is embodying the teachings of the Quran and the Sunnah in all aspects of life. Imam al-Haddad, in *The Book of Assistance*, emphasizes the importance of balancing ritual worship with moral conduct, social responsibility, and the cultivation of good character. This chapter explores key elements of Islamic practice, including ritual prayer, zakat, fasting, Hajj, prayer in congregation, scrupulousness, enjoining good and forbidding evil, kindness, charity, following the Sunnah, and good character.

2.1 Ritual Prayer (Salah): The Foundation of Worship

Ritual prayer (*Salah*) is the second pillar of Islam and the most vital act of worship in a Muslim's daily life. It serves as a direct link between the believer and Allah, reinforcing faith, discipline, and mindfulness. Imam al-Haddad, in *The Book of Assistance*, emphasizes the importance of perfecting *Salah*, observing it regularly, and performing it with presence of heart.

The Quran highlights the centrality of prayer: "Indeed, prayer has been decreed upon the believers a decree of specified times." (Quran, An-Nisa 4:103)

The Importance of Salah

- **A Pillar of Islam:** The Prophet Muhammad (peace and blessings be upon him) said:
  "The first thing for which a person will be brought to account on the Day of Judgment is the prayer. If it is sound, the rest of his deeds will

be sound; and if it is corrupt, the rest of his deeds will be corrupt."
(Tirmidhi)

- **Connection with Allah:** *Salah* is a daily opportunity to renew one's covenant with Allah and seek His guidance and forgiveness.

- **Purification of the Soul:** Through *Salah*, a believer regularly detaches from worldly distractions, focusing on the remembrance of Allah.

The Elements of Salah

Outer Dimensions of Salah
- **Performing Wudu':** Ensure ritual purity before standing in prayer, as Allah says:
  "O you who have believed, when you rise to [perform] prayer, wash your faces and your forearms to the elbows..." (Quran, Al-Ma'idah 5:6)

- **Observing the Correct Times:** Pray each *Salah* within its prescribed time, as delaying without valid reason can lead to sin.

- **Facing the Qibla:** Stand in the direction of the Ka'aba in Makkah, symbolizing unity and focus in worship.

- **Physical Actions:** Perform the bowing (*Ruku'*), prostration (*Sujood*), and all other movements with calmness and proper form.

Inner Dimensions of Salah
- **Presence of Heart:** Focus solely on Allah, striving to free the mind from distractions.

- **Sincerity (*Ikhlas*):** Perform *Salah* seeking only Allah's pleasure, not for show or worldly recognition.

- **Contemplation:** Reflect on the meanings of the Quranic verses and supplications recited during prayer.

The Prophet (peace and blessings be upon him) said:
"Pray as if you see Allah, and if you do not see Him, know that He sees you."
(Sahih Bukhari; Sahih Muslim)

The Rewards of Salah

- **Forgiveness of Sins:** The Prophet (peace and blessings be upon him) said:
"When a Muslim performs wudu' properly and then prays two rak'ahs with full concentration, his past sins are forgiven."
(Sahih Bukhari)

- **A Source of Light:** Allah says:
"Establish prayer, for prayer restrains one from shameful and unjust deeds." (Quran, Al-Ankabut 29:45)

- **Closeness to Allah:** The Prophet (peace and blessings be upon him) said:
"The closest a servant is to his Lord is when he is in prostration, so increase your supplications." (Sahih Muslim)

Practical Tips to Perfect Salah

- **Prepare Spiritually and Physically:** Make *wudu'* with focus, wear clean clothing, and ensure your prayer space is tidy and quiet.

- **Pray in Congregation:** Aim to pray at the mosque, especially for Fajr and Isha, as the reward is significantly multiplied.

- **Focus on Quality, Not Just Quantity:** It is better to pray fewer rak'ahs with concentration than many without mindfulness.

- **Recite Supplications and Dhikr After Salah:** These enhance the spiritual benefits of prayer. For example:

  ○ Tasbih (33x SubhanAllah, 33x Alhamdulillah, 33x Allahu Akbar, and 1x La ilaha illa Allah).

Sunnah and Voluntary Prayers

- **Sunnah Mu'akkadah (Emphasized Sunnah Prayers):**

  ○ 2 rak'ahs before Fajr, 4 before Dhuhr, 2 after Dhuhr, 2 after Maghrib, and 2 after Isha.

- **Salat al-Duha (Forenoon Prayer):** Prayed after sunrise, it brings immense rewards. The Prophet (peace and blessings be upon him) said: "In the morning, charity is due on every joint of the body... Two rak'ahs offered in the forenoon suffice for that." (Sahih Muslim)

- **Tahajjud (Night Prayer):** Performed in the last third of the night, this prayer is a means of attaining closeness to Allah. Allah praises those who perform it: "They arise from [their] beds; they supplicate their Lord in fear and aspiration..." (Quran, As-Sajdah 32:16)

Neglecting Salah: A Grave Warning

Imam al-Haddad cautions against neglecting *Salah*, as it is a defining act of faith. Allah warns: "But there came after them successors who neglected prayer and pursued desires; so they are going to meet evil." (Quran, Maryam 19:59)

The Prophet (peace and blessings be upon him) said:
"The covenant between us and them is prayer; whoever abandons it has disbelieved." (Sunan al-Tirmidhi, Hasan Sahih)

Ritual prayer (*Salah*) is the cornerstone of a Muslim's spiritual life, serving as a reminder of Allah's presence and mercy throughout the day. Imam al-Haddad's teachings stress the importance of both the outer and inner dimensions of *Salah*, urging believers to approach it with sincerity, focus, and discipline. By perfecting *Salah*, praying in congregation, and integrating voluntary prayers, a believer fulfills their duty to Allah and reap immense rewards in this life and the Hereafter.

2.2 Zakat: Purifying Wealth and Soul

Zakat is a mandatory act of charity and a pillar of Islam. It purifies wealth and nurtures compassion for the less fortunate. Allah commands: "Take from their wealth a charity by which you purify them and cause them to increase, and invoke [Allah's blessings] upon them." (Quran, At-Tawbah 9:103).

Social and Spiritual Benefits

- **Purification of Wealth:** It removes greed and selfishness from the heart.

- **Bridging Inequality:** Zakat strengthens societal bonds by supporting the needy.

- **Earning Allah's Reward:** Allah promises blessings for those who fulfill this duty.

2.3 Fasting: A Shield for the Believer

Fasting, especially during Ramadan, is an act of worship that trains the soul in discipline, patience, and God-consciousness. Allah says: "O you who have believed, decreed upon you is fasting as it was decreed upon those before you that you may become righteous."
(Quran, Al-Baqarah 2:183)

Spiritual Dimensions

- **Taming the Nafs (Lower Self):** Fasting subdues desires and cultivates self-control.

- **Renewing Gratitude:** Experiencing hunger fosters appreciation for Allah's blessings.

- **Drawing Closer to Allah:** It increases taqwa (God-consciousness), the essence of faith.

The Prophet (peace and blessings be upon him) said: "Fastng is a shield. So when one of you is fasting, he should not behave foolishly or argue. If someone curses him or fights with him, let him say: 'I am fasting.'" (Sahih al-Bukhari; Sahih Muslim)

Voluntary Fasts

- Six days of Shawwal: Equivalent to fasting for the whole year.

- Mondays and Thursdays: Days of presenting deeds to Allah.

- The Day of Arafah: Expiates sins for two years.

- The Day of Ashura: Expiates sins for one year.

2.4 Hajj: A Journey of Submission

Hajj (pilgrimage) is a physical and spiritual journey that symbolizes submission and unity. Allah commands: "And proclaim to the people the Hajj [pilgrimage]; they will come to you on foot and on every lean camel; they will come from every distant pass." (Quran, Al-Hajj 22:27)

Key Rituals and Their Meanings

- **Ihram:** A state of equality and humility before Allah.

- **Tawaf:** Circling the Kaaba represents devotion to Allah as the center of life.

- **Standing at Arafah:** A day of profound supplication and mercy.

- **Sacrifice:** Reflecting on the story of Prophet Ibrahim (peace be upon him) and submission to Allah.

The Prophet (peace and blessings be upon him) said: "Whoever performs Hajj and does not commit any obscenity or wrongdoing will come out as sinless as the day his mother gave birth to him." (Sahih Bukhari; Sahih Muslim)

2.5 Prayer in Congregation: A Pillar of Unity and Community

Prayer in congregation is central to Islamic worship, fostering unity, discipline, and mutual support among believers. Imam al-Haddad emphasizes the profound spiritual and social benefits of performing prayers in congregation, urging Muslims to prioritize it, especially for obligatory prayers in the mosque.

The Prophet Muhammad (peace and blessings be upon him) said: "Prayer in congregation is twenty-seven times more rewarding than prayer performed alone." (Sahih al-Bukhari; Sahih Muslim)

The Spiritual Significance of Congregational Prayer

- **Increased Reward:** Praying in congregation multiplies the reward significantly, as stated in the hadith above.

- **Unity of the Ummah:** Standing shoulder to shoulder fosters equality, unity, and a sense of belonging among Muslims.

- **Divine Blessings and Protection:** Congregational prayers invite Allah's mercy and protect us from trials and distractions.

- **Accountability and Consistency:** Regular attendance at congregational prayers encourages discipline and helps believers maintain their connection with Allah.

The Role of the Masjid

The masjid serves as the heart of the Muslim community, a place of worship, learning, and social interaction. Imam al-Haddad stresses the importance of frequenting the masjid and performing prayers there, particularly for men. Allah says: "In houses [of worship] which Allah has ordered to be raised and that His name be mentioned therein; exalting Him within them in the morning and the evenings are men whom neither commerce nor sale distracts from the remembrance of Allah." (Quran, An-Noor 24:36-37)

Etiquette of Congregational Prayer

- **Purity and Cleanliness:** Perform wudu' before heading to the mosque and ensure you are in a state of physical and spiritual purity.

- **Arrive Early:** Try to reach the mosque before the call to prayer (*adhan*), allowing time for additional prayers or dhikr.

- **Maintain Order and Discipline:** Follow the imam attentively and avoid any actions that disrupt the harmony of the congregation.

- **Recite Supplications:** Upon entering the mosque, recite: "Allahumma iftah li abwaba rahmatika" (O Allah, open for me the doors of Your mercy.) (Sahih Muslim, 713)

Benefits of the Congregational Prayer

- **Erasing Sins:** The Prophet (peace and blessings be upon him) said: "When a man performs wudu' perfectly, then goes to the mosque with the sole intention of praying, for every step he takes, one sin is erased, one rank is raised, and one good deed is recorded for him." (Sahih Muslim)

- **Angelic Presence:** Angels pray for those who wait for the prayer in the mosque, as narrated in a hadith:
  "The angels continue to supplicate for one of you as long as he remains in the place where he prayed, saying: 'O Allah, forgive him; O Allah, have mercy on him.'" (Sahih Bukhari; Sahih Muslim)

- **Social Bonding:** Praying in the congregation strengthens community ties, as worshippers meet regularly, check on each other, and build bonds of brotherhood.

Encouragement for Consistency in Congregation

Imam al-Haddad reminds believers of the grave loss of neglecting congregational prayer without a valid excuse. The Prophet (peace and blessings be upon him) said: "By Him in Whose Hand is my soul! I considered ordering firewood to be collected and then commanding the call to prayer to be made. Then I would appoint a man to lead the people in prayer and go to the men who did not attend and burn their houses down on them." (Sahih Bukhari; Sahih Muslim). This hadith underscores the seriousness of attending congregational prayers, especially for men.

Special Emphasis on Fajr and Isha

The Prophet Muhammad (peace and blessings be upon him) highlighted the importance of Fajr and Isha prayers in the congregation:
"The most burdensome prayers for the hypocrites are the Isha and Fajr prayers. If they knew the rewards for them, they would attend them even if they had to crawl." (Sahih Bukhari; Sahih Muslim)

Prayer in congregation is not just an individual act of worship but a collective experience that unites the Muslim community and strengthens its spiritual and social fabric. Imam al-Haddad's teachings remind believers of the immense rewards and benefits of praying in congregation, urging them to make it a regular part of their lives. By attending the masjid, fostering unity, and encouraging others to join, believers fulfill their duties toward Allah and the community, achieving blessings in both this world and the Hereafter.

2.6 Scrupulousness (Wara'): Avoiding Doubtful Matters

Scrupulousness, or *wara'*, involves avoiding not only haram (forbidden) but also doubtful or excessive halal (permissible) matters. The Prophet (peace and blessings be upon him) said: "The halal is clear, and the haram is clear, and between them are doubtful matters which many people do not know. So, whoever avoids doubtful matters has preserved their religion and their honor." (Sahih Bukhari; Sahih Muslim)

Example of the Companions

The scrupulousness of the Companions set an unparalleled standard. It is reported: "A Companion of the Prophet would abandon seventy permissible matters out of fear that they might lead to something forbidden." (Ibn Rajab al-Hanbali, Jami' al-'Ulum wa'l-Hikam)

How to Cultivate Wara'

- **Avoid Doubtful Actions:** Refrain from ambiguous matters to ensure your actions remain pure.

- **Develop Taqwa:** Strengthen your awareness of Allah in all decisions.

- **Seek Knowledge:** Learn Islamic rulings to discern between permissible and impermissible.

2.7 Enjoining Good and Forbidding Evil

Enjoining good and forbidding evil is a collective responsibility that sustains the moral fabric of society. Allah says: "You are the best nation produced [as an example] for mankind. You enjoin what is right and forbid what is wrong and believe in Allah." (Quran, Aal-E-Imran 3:110)

Principles of Enjoining Good

- **Knowledge:** Ensure you understand what you advocate.

- **Wisdom and Patience:** Approach others gently and respectfully.

- **Prioritize:** Focus on significant issues before minor ones.

The Prophet (peace and blessings be upon him) said: "Whoever among you sees an evil, let him change it with his hand. If he cannot, then with his tongue. If he cannot, then with his heart – and that is the weakest of faith." (Sahih Muslim)

This duty sustains the moral fabric of society. Allah says: "Let there be [arising] from you a nation inviting to [all that is] good, enjoining what is right and forbidding what is wrong, and those will be the successful." (Quran, Aal-E-Imran, 3:104)

The Prophet (peace and blessings be upon him) said: "Whoever among you sees an evil, let him change it with his hand. If he cannot, then with his tongue. If he cannot, then with his heart—and that is the weakest of faith." (Sahih Muslim)

2.8 Kindness and Charity

Kindness and charity are central to living Islam, reflecting Allah's mercy and generosity. The Quran states: "Indeed, Allah commands justice, good conduct, and giving to relatives." (Quran, An-Nahl, 16:90)

Forms of Charity

- **Zakat and Sadaqah:** Financial help for the needy.

- **Non-Material Acts:** Smiling, giving good advice, and assisting others.

- **Caring for Creation:** Protecting animals and the environment.

The Prophet (peace and blessings be upon him) said: "Every act of kindness is charity." (Sahih Bukhari)

2.9 Following the Sunnah: Emulating the Prophet

The Sunnah provides a practical guide to living Islam. Allah commands: "Say, [O Muhammad], 'If you should love Allah, then follow me, so Allah will love you and forgive you your sins.'" (Quran, Aal-E-Imran, 3:31)

2.10 Good Character: The Pinnacle of Faith

Good character is the essence of Islam. The Prophet (peace and blessings be upon him) said: "The most beloved of you to me and the closest to me on the Day of Judgment are those of you who are best in character." (Sunan At-Tirmidhi, Hasan Sahih)

Key Traits to Cultivate

- **Patience:** Persevere in hardship and avoid anger.

- **Humility:** Recognize one's dependence on Allah.

- **Gratitude:** Express thankfulness for Allah's blessings.

Conclusion

Living Islam involves harmonizing acts of worship with ethical conduct and social responsibility. By embodying the teachings of the Quran and the Sunnah, believers can attain Allah's pleasure, strengthen their communities, and achieve success in this world and the Hereafter. Imam al-Haddad's guidance serves as a roadmap for those striving to live a life of devotion, integrity, and excellence.

CHAPTER THREE

Avoiding Sins: A Path to Spiritual Purity and Fulfillment

I n Islam, avoiding sins is a cornerstone of faith and a critical component of maintaining a close relationship with Allah. Sins not only harm one's soul but also obstruct spiritual growth, damage relationships, and create a barrier between a person and Allah. The Quran and Hadith provide clear guidance on identifying sins, understanding their consequences, and seeking repentance. This chapter explores the concept of sin, its various categories, the impact of sins on the individual and society, sins of the limbs, and practical strategies for avoiding them.

3.1 Understanding the Concept of Sin in Islam

Definition of Sin

In Islam, sin is defined as any thought, word, or action that contradicts Allah's commands and the teachings of the Prophet Muhammad (peace and blessings be upon him). Sins violate the moral, ethical, and spiritual principles set by Allah to guide humanity toward righteousness and success. The Quran states, "And do not approach unlawful sexual intercourse. Indeed, it is ever an immorality and is evil as a way" (Quran, Al-Isra' 17:32), illustrating how specific actions are forbidden for the well-being of individuals and society.

Sin as a Barrier to Allah

Sins create a spiritual barrier, distancing individuals from Allah and disrupting their sense of inner peace. The Quran describes this:
"No! Rather, the stain has covered their hearts of that which they were earning" (Quran, Al-Mutaffifin 83:14).
Repeated sins tarnish the heart, making it resistant to divine guidance and spiritual light. This results in feelings of emptiness, anxiety, and dissatisfaction as the connection with Allah is weakened.

Accountability Before Allah

Islam emphasizes individual accountability for all actions, big or small. The Quran states:
"Whoever does an atom's weight of good will see it, and whoever does an atom's weight of evil will see it" (Quran, Al-Zalzala 99:7-8).
This awareness motivates believers to act with mindfulness, knowing they will stand before Allah on the Day of Judgment to answer for their deeds.

Allah's Mercy and Forgiveness

Despite human fallibility, Allah's mercy is vast and boundless. He promises forgiveness to those who repent sincerely:
"Say, 'O My servants who have transgressed against themselves, do not despair of the mercy of Allah. Indeed, Allah forgives all sins'" (Quran, Az-Zumar 39:53).
This assurance serves as a source of hope, encouraging believers to seek forgiveness and strive to improve.

3.2 Categories of Sins in Islam

In Islamic teachings, sins are generally divided into two main categories: major sins (*kaba'ir*) and minor sins (*sagha'ir*). Understanding the nature of these sins helps Muslims take measures to avoid them and seek repentance when necessary.

Major Sins (Kaba'ir):

- Major sins are grave violations that carry severe consequences in this life and the Hereafter. These sins are explicitly prohibited in the Quran and Hadith, and their seriousness is emphasized by Allah and the Prophet

Muhammad (peace and blessings be upon him). Engaging in a major sin without repentance is considered a grave matter.

- **Examples of Major Sins**:

  - **Shirk (Associating Partners with Allah)**: Shirk is considered the greatest sin in Islam, as it denies the oneness of Allah. Allah says, "Indeed, Allah does not forgive associating others with Him [shirk], but He forgives what is less than that for whom He wills" (Quran, An-Nisa 4:48). Shirk involves worshipping other beings or objects alongside Allah and undermines the core tenet of Islam: Tawhid (belief in the oneness of Allah).

  - **Murder**: Taking the life of another unjustly is a major sin. The Quran states, "Whoever kills a soul unless for a soul or corruption [done] in the land - it is as if he had slain mankind entirely" (Quran, Al-Ma'ida 5:32). Islam holds the sanctity of life in high regard, and taking a life unjustly is seen as an act of extreme transgression.

  - **Disrespect to Parents**: Islam emphasizes honoring and respecting parents, and being disrespectful or unkind to them is considered a major sin. The Prophet (peace and blessings be upon him) said, "Shall I not inform you about the biggest of the major sins? They said, 'Yes, O Allah's Messenger.' He said, 'To join partners in worship with Allah, to be undutiful to one's parents'" (Sahih Bukhari).

  - **False Witness/Testimony**: Bearing false witness or lying under oath is a major sin in Islam because it harms others and distorts justice. The Prophet (peace and blessings be upon him) warned, "Avoid the seven destructive sins" and included false testimony among them (Sahih Bukhari; Sahih Muslim).

  - **Consuming Interest (Riba)**: Charging or paying interest is forbidden in Islam due to its exploitative nature. The Quran states, "Allah has permitted trade and has forbidden interest" (Quran, Al-Baqarah 2:275).

  - **Engaging in Magic**: Practicing magic or sorcery is forbidden in Islam as it involves harm, deception, and reliance on means other than Allah.

- Major sins require sincere repentance, including regret, seeking Allah's forgiveness, and, in many cases, making amends or undoing harm caused by the sin.

Minor Sins (Sagha'ir):

* Minor sins are less severe than major sins. They include everyday mistakes or small missteps in thoughts, speech, or actions. While they are not as grave as major sins, they still require repentance and should be avoided as much as possible.

* Minor sins include using harsh words, harboring negative thoughts, minor dishonesty, neglecting small acts of kindness, and failing to perform recommended worship. Allah more easily forgives minor sins, especially when good deeds follow them.

* The Prophet Muhammad (peace and blessings be upon him) said, "The five daily prayers, Friday to Friday, and Ramadan to Ramadan expiate what is between them, as long as one avoids major sins." (Muslim). This hadith highlights that minor sins are often forgiven through regular acts of worship and good deeds.

Hidden Sins (Sins of the Heart):

* Islam also recognizes hidden sins, meaning sins that exist internally within the heart rather than through physical actions. These include arrogance, envy, pride, hypocrisy, and hatred. Although these sins may not be outwardly visible, they corrupt the soul and lead to further misdeeds.

* **Examples**:

    ○ **Arrogance (*Kibr*)**: The Prophet Muhammad (peace and blessings be upon him) said, "No one who has an atom's weight of arrogance in his heart will enter Paradise" (Muslim). Arrogance is a sin of the heart that prevents humility, gratitude, and sincere worship.

    ○ **Envy (Hasad)**: Envy is disliking that others receive blessings and wishing that they lose them. The Quran advises against envy: "And do not wish for that by which Allah has made some of you exceed others" (Quran, An-Nisa 4:32). Envy breeds dissatisfaction and can lead to harmful behavior toward others.

- ○ **Hypocrisy (Nifaq)**: Hypocrisy is the act of pretending to believe in Islam while secretly disbelieving or acting contrary to one's professed beliefs. The Quran and Hadith describe hypocrisy as a dangerous state that deceives others and brings harm to one's own soul.

Sins Against Others (Huquq al-Ibad):

- Islam places great importance on respecting others' rights. Sins against others include actions like dishonesty, betrayal, theft, lying, and failing to fulfill promises. These sins not only harm the person committing them but also inflict damage on others.

- When a sin involves another person's rights, repentance includes seeking forgiveness from Allah and making amends or seeking forgiveness from the affected person. Islam emphasizes that rights between individuals must be resolved before Allah fully forgives them.

The Prophet Muhammad (peace and blessings be upon him) specifically warned Muslims to avoid seven grave sins known as the "seven destructive sins" (*al-mubiqat*). These sins are considered especially harmful to both individuals and society, as they lead to severe spiritual, moral, and social consequences. In this chapter, we'll take a closer look at each of these destructive sins, exploring their significance and why Islam strongly emphasizes avoiding them.

3.3 Sins of the Limbs

The limbs are entrusted by Allah to carry out righteous deeds, but they can also commit sins when misused. Recognizing and avoiding these sins is critical for spiritual health.

Sins of the Tongue

The tongue is one of the most frequently misused limbs, as words can cause immense harm. Examples include:
- **Lying:** "Cursed are the liars" (Quran, AleImran 3:61).

- **Backbiting (Ghibah):** Described in the Quran as eating the flesh of a dead brother (Quran, Al-Hujurat 49:12).

- **Slander:** False accusations destroy reputations and social trust.

Sins of the Eyes

The eyes can lead to sin by looking at prohibited things, such as immodest images or envying others' blessings. The Quran commands:
"Tell the believing men to lower their gaze and guard their private parts" (Quran, An-Noor 24:30).

Sins of the Ears

Listening to gossip, slander, or immoral content corrupts the heart and distracts from Allah's remembrance. Believers are urged to avoid such harmful practices.

Sins of the Hands

The hands can commit sins such as theft, physical harm, or consuming unlawful wealth. The Quran warns against using one's hands to oppress or harm others.

Sins of the Feet

The feet can lead a person toward sinful places or away from fulfilling obligations. For example, avoiding congregational prayer without valid reasons is considered sinful.

Sins of the Private Parts

Guarding chastity is emphasized in Islam. The Quran states: "And those who guard their chastity—except with their wives or those their right hands possess" (Quran, Mu'minun 23:5-6). Adultery and fornication are grave sins explicitly condemned in Quran. "And do not approach unlawful sexual intercourse. Indeed, it is ever an immorality and is evil as a way." (Quran, Al-Isra' 17:32).

3.4 The Seven Destructive Sins

The Prophet Muhammad (peace and blessings be upon him) said, "Avoid the seven destructive sins." The companions asked, "O Messenger of Allah, what are they?" He replied, "Associating others with Allah (shirk), witchcraft (sihr), killing a soul whom Allah has forbidden to kill except by right, consuming interest (riba), consuming the property of orphans, fleeing from the battlefield, and slandering chaste, innocent, believing women." (Sahih Bukhari; Sahih Muslim)

Each of these sins violates essential principles of Islamic teachings and causes significant harm to individuals and society. Each of these sins disrupts societal harmony and weakens the bond between individuals and Allah. Let's look at each one in detail:

Shirk (Associating Others with Allah): Contradicts Tawhid, the foundation of Islamic faith.

Shirk, or associating partners with Allah, is considered the greatest sin in Islam. It undermines the core belief of *Tawhid* (the oneness of Allah) and goes against the very foundation of the Islamic faith. Shirk can take many forms, including worshipping other deities, relying on anyone or anything as equal to Allah, or attributing divine qualities to creation.

- **Why Shirk is Destructive**: Shirk fundamentally breaks the bond between a person and Allah. Allah says in the Quran, "Indeed, Allah does not forgive association with Him, but He forgives what is less than that for whom He wills" (Quran, An-Nisa 4:48). Associating others with Allah leads to spiritual ruin, and if not repented for, can prevent a person from entering paradise.

- **Examples of Shirk**: Worshipping idols, believing in other gods, or relying on charms and superstitions as if they have divine power.

Practicing Witchcraft (Sihr): Manipulates others and introduces elements of shirk.

Sihr, or engaging in witchcraft and sorcery, involves attempting to control or influence events and people through supernatural means, often invoking forces other than Allah. Islam strongly condemns *sihr* as it seeks power beyond what Allah has permitted, often resulting in harm and deception.

- **Why Witchcraft is Destructive**: Sorcery and witchcraft can harm others physically, emotionally, and spiritually, while promoting dependency on forces other than Allah. This act contradicts the principles of trust and reliance on Allah (*tawakkul*) and introduces elements of shirk.

- **Examples of Witchcraft**: Casting spells, attempting to manipulate others with supernatural methods, using talismans, and seeking assistance from jinn or spirits.

Unjust Killing: Opposes justice and the sanctity of life.

Islam places immense value on the sanctity of life, and taking an innocent life unjustly is one of the most serious crimes in Islam. Killing without a just cause is seen as an attack on humanity as a whole. Allah says in the Quran, "Whoever kills a soul unless for a soul or for corruption [done] in the land—it is as if he had slain mankind entirely" (Quran, Al-Ma'ida 5:32).

- **Why Killing is Destructive**: Taking a life without just cause not only harms the victim but also devastates families, disrupts society, and corrupts communities. This sin is directly opposed to Islam's teachings on justice and compassion.

- **Examples of Unjust Killing**: Murdering someone out of anger, jealousy, or revenge or taking a life without due process or a valid, lawful reason.

Consuming Interest (Riba): Exploits the vulnerable and fosters inequality.

Interest, or *riba*, refers to unjustly profiting from loans or capital without engaging in productive work. Islam prohibits the charging or paying of interest, as it often leads to exploitation, creates economic imbalances, and oppresses the poor.

- **Why Riba is Destructive**: Interest-based transactions create inequality and injustice within society, favoring the wealthy while trapping others in debt. Allah warns against riba, stating, "Allah has permitted trade and has forbidden interest" (Quran, AL-Baqarah 2:275). Those who engage in riba are warned of severe consequences both in this life and the Hereafter.

- **Examples of Riba**: Charging interest on loans, receiving interest from bank accounts, or engaging in transactions where profit is gained without productive work or value creation.

Consuming Orphans' Wealth: Exploits the most vulnerable members of society.

In Islam, orphans are specially protected, and their welfare is emphasized in both the Quran and Hadith. Taking advantage of an orphan's vulnerability by consuming their property unjustly is seen as a serious offense. The Quran states, "Indeed, those who devour the property of orphans unjustly are only consuming into their bellies fire." (Quran, An-Nisa 4:10).

- **Why This Sin is Destructive**: Orphans are among the most vulnerable members of society, and exploiting their wealth is not only unjust but deeply harmful. Such actions reflect greed and heartlessness and violate the trust Allah has placed upon guardians.

- **Examples of Consuming Orphans' Wealth**: Misusing orphans' inheritance, diverting funds intended for their care, or taking advantage of their property.

Fleeing the Battlefield: Betrays one's community and weakens collective defense.

In Islamic teachings, courage, sacrifice, and standing for justice are highly valued. Fleeing from the battlefield in times of just conflict, especially when defending one's faith or community, is considered a major sin. It demonstrates cowardice and can lead to the defeat and suffering of one's people.

- **Why This Sin is Destructive**: Deserting one's duty not only betrays one's companions but also weakens the community and puts others in danger. Islam emphasizes unity, loyalty, and selflessness, especially in times of defense.

- **Examples of This Sin**: Fleeing in battle for personal gain, abandoning one's post in a just cause, or refusing to stand up for justice when necessary.

Slandering Chaste Women: Causes social discord and emotional harm.

Slandering, particularly against chaste women, is a serious offense in Islam. False accusations against women concerning their chastity lead to harm, damage reputations, and disrupt social harmony. Islam upholds the dignity and honor of every individual and requires evidence before accusations of immorality.

- **Why This Sin is Destructive**: Slandering an innocent person, especially concerning matters of chastity, can destroy lives, tear apart families, and cause emotional distress. Islam seeks to protect personal honor and prohibits unfounded accusations, promoting justice and respect for others.

- **Examples of This Sin**: Accusing a woman of adultery or other immoral behavior without evidence, spreading rumors or false claims, and defaming others.

3.5 Consequences of Sins

Spiritual Consequences

Sins darken the heart, as described in the Hadith: "When a servant commits a sin, a black spot forms on their heart. If they repent, it is removed. If they persist, it spreads until their heart is completely blackened" (Sahih Muslim).

Social Consequences

Sins such as dishonesty and oppression erode trust, create discord, and harm the moral fabric of society. A community plagued by sin loses its sense of justice and compassion.

The Day of Judgment

On the Day of Judgment, every deed will be weighed, and no act, however small, will be overlooked (Quran, 99:7-8).

3.6 Strategies to Avoid Sin

- **Seek Knowledge:** Understanding sins and their consequences fosters mindfulness and strengthens resolve.

- **Engage in Worship:** Regular prayer, fasting, and dhikr purify the heart and shield against sinful inclinations.

- **Repent Regularly:** Sincere repentance erases sins and renews one's commitment to righteousness.

- **Surround Yourself with Righteous Company:** Good friends inspire virtuous behavior and discourage sin.

- **Set Boundaries:** Avoid situations or influences that encourage sinful behavior, such as harmful media or negative environments.

Conclusion

Avoiding sins is essential for personal spiritual growth and societal harmony. By understanding sins, their categories, and their impact, believers can strive to protect their souls and cultivate a stronger connection with Allah. Muslims can work toward a life of righteousness, peace, and ultimate success in the Hereafter through regular worship, sincere repentance, and conscious effort to avoid sinful actions.

CHAPTER FOUR

Zuhd (Indifference to the Dunya): Embracing Detachment for a Purposeful Life

In Islam, *zuhd*, or indifference to the *dunya* (worldly life), is a fundamental principle that encourages believers to focus on the eternal life of the Hereafter rather than becoming overly attached to temporary worldly pleasures. Zuhd is not about rejecting the world altogether or living in extreme deprivation; rather, it's about maintaining a healthy detachment from material wealth, social status, and physical comforts, recognizing them as fleeting. This chapter explores the concept of zuhd, its role in achieving a balanced life, and how it fosters spiritual growth, contentment, and a sense of purpose.

4.1 Understanding Zuhd: Indifference, Not Rejection

Zuhd is often misunderstood as a call to abandon all worldly goods and lead an ascetic life. However, Islam's understanding of zuhd is more nuanced. It is not about rejecting the blessings Allah has provided but about using them wisely without becoming enslaved by them. The goal of *zuhd* is to cultivate a heart that is attached to Allah, not to possessions, status, or fleeting pleasures.

What Zuhd Is and Is Not:

- *Zuhd* does not mean abandoning wealth or avoiding one's responsibilities. Instead, it means not allowing wealth or worldly pursuits to dominate one's heart. It's about using what is needed, being grateful for Allah's blessings, and knowing that one's true worth is not defined by material possessions.

- The Quran and Hadith emphasize moderation. Allah says, "And seek, through that which Allah has given you, the home of the Hereafter; and yet, do not forget your share of the world" (Quran, Al-Qasas 28:77). This ayah reminds believers that while pursuing a comfortable life is acceptable, it should not be at the cost of one's relationship with Allah or the pursuit of spiritual growth.

Prophetic Teachings on Zuhd:

- The Prophet Muhammad (peace and blessings be upon him) is the ultimate model of *zuhd*. Despite his high status as the Messenger of Allah (peace and blessings be upon him), he lived a simple life, often choosing modest clothing, food, and shelter. He demonstrated that true contentment comes from a heart free from attachment to worldly things.

- The Prophet (peace and blessings be upon him) said, "Wealth is not in having many possessions. Rather, true wealth is the richness of the soul." (Muslim). This statement emphasizes that true richness comes from spiritual contentment rather than material abundance.

4.2 The Spiritual Benefits of Zuhd

Zuhd offers numerous spiritual benefits that help believers align their lives with their ultimate purpose—pleasing Allah and preparing for the Hereafter. Detachment from worldly attachments enables a deeper connection with Allah, increases gratitude, and fosters a sense of peace and satisfaction that transcends material circumstances.

Cultivating Inner Peace:

- One of the main benefits of *zuhd* is the inner peace that comes from not being constantly entangled in desires and worries about material possessions. A person practicing *zuhd* is free from the anxiety that comes with pursuing wealth and status, allowing their heart to find tranquility in remembrance of Allah.

- This peace is rooted in contentment (*qana'ah*)—being satisfied with what one has and accepting Allah's provision. The Prophet (peace and blessings be upon him) said, "Be content with what Allah has given you, and you will be the richest of people." (Ibn Majah). Contentment brings calmness and protects the heart from greed, envy, and constant dissatisfaction.

Strengthening Tawakkul (Reliance on Allah):

- When a believer practices zuhd, they naturally develop a stronger sense of *tawakkul* (reliance on Allah). By focusing less on accumulating wealth or securing social status, they place their trust in Allah as their Provider, Protector, and Sustainer. This reliance on Allah fortifies faith and fosters a deep sense of security that cannot be shaken by external circumstances.

- The Quran states, "And whoever relies upon Allah—then He is sufficient for him." (Quran, At-Talaq 65:3). This ayah encourages believers to detach from worldly attachments and rely solely on Allah, knowing that He will provide for their needs.

Fostering Gratitude:

- *Zuhd* also encourages gratitude. When believers are content with what they have, they are more likely to appreciate the blessings in their lives and recognize them as gifts from Allah. This gratitude, in turn, strengthens their relationship with Allah, as they see Him as the source of all goodness.

- Gratitude enhances one's spiritual state, making one more mindful of Allah's generosity and kindness toward others. It fosters a positive outlook and reduces feelings of inadequacy, leading to a more fulfilling life rooted in appreciation.

4.3 Zuhd in Daily Life: Practical Steps to Detach from the Dunya

Practicing *zuhd* doesn't mean abandoning one's career, family, or possessions. Instead, it involves adjusting one's mindset and focusing on the Hereafter while engaging in worldly activities. The following are practical steps for cultivating *zuhd* in daily life.

Prioritize Intentions:

- Intentions are the foundation of every action in Islam. Setting a sincere intention before engaging in any activity allows Muslims to align their actions with their purpose. Whether working, studying, or spending time with family, if done with the intention of pleasing Allah, these actions can become acts of worship and contribute to one's spiritual growth.

- The Prophet (peace and blessings be upon him) said, "Be content with what Allah has given you, and you will be the richest of people." (Ibn Majah). Contentment brings calmness and protects the heart from greed, envy, and constant dissatisfaction. said, "Actions are judged by intentions, and every person will get what they intended." (Bukhari). This hadith reminds believers that their intentions determine the value of their actions. By setting intentions that focus on serving Allah, Muslims can maintain a balance between worldly pursuits and spiritual goals.

Limit Material Desires:

- Practicing *zuhd* means not giving in to every material desire. Limiting spending on unnecessary items, avoiding excessive indulgence in luxury, and resisting the urge to upgrade possessions help foster contentment and gratitude constantly.

- This restraint does not mean depriving oneself but rather learning to appreciate the simplicity of life. The Prophet Muhammad (peace and blessings be upon him) said, "Be content with what Allah has given you, and you will be the richest of people." (Ibn Majah). Contentment brings calmness and protects the heart from greed, envy, and constant dissatisfaction. demonstrated this when he said, "Be in this world as though you were a stranger or a traveler" (Bukhari). This mindset encourages believers to view worldly possessions as temporary and focus on preparing for the Hereafter.

Engage in Charity and Generosity:

- One effective way to detach from material possessions is through charity and generosity. Giving to others reminds Muslims that wealth is a trust from Allah, and that they have a responsibility to help those in need. Acts of charity reduce attachment to wealth and reinforce the understanding that all resources ultimately belong to Allah.

- The Prophet Muhammad (peace and blessings be upon him) said, "Charity does not decrease wealth" (Muslim). This hadith encourages believers to give generously, as Allah promises to bless and replenish what is given in charity.

Spend Time in Reflection and Worship:

- Practicing *zuhd* requires regular reflection and worship, which help believers stay grounded and focused on the Hereafter. Taking time for *dhikr* (remembrance of Allah), *Du'a* (supplication), and *Salah* (prayer) keeps the heart connected to Allah and distances it from worldly attachments.

- Reflection on death, the temporary nature of life, and the reality of the Hereafter also reinforces the need to prioritize spiritual pursuits over material gain. By remembering that everything in this world is temporary, believers are more likely to focus on what truly matters.

4.5 Zuhd as a Path to Purposeful Living

Zuhd leads to a more purposeful life by encouraging believers to focus on spiritual growth, personal integrity, and compassionate service to others. Detaching from the excesses of the *Dunya* allows Muslims to lead lives that are meaningful, impactful, and centered on their ultimate purpose: worshipping Allah and preparing for the Hereafter.

Living with Sincerity and Integrity:

- *Zuhd* enables believers to lead lives of sincerity and integrity. When material pursuits no longer dominate, individuals can focus on building character, fulfilling responsibilities, and making decisions based on Islamic principles rather than worldly gain.

- A person who practices *zuhd* is less likely to be swayed by greed, dishonesty, or selfish ambitions. This commitment to sincerity strengthens their relationship with Allah and serves as an example to others, embodying the principles of Islam in daily life.

Finding Fulfillment Beyond Wealth:

- In a world that often equates success with wealth, *zuhd* reminds believers that true fulfillment comes from spiritual contentment, not material abundance. Those who practice *zuhd* find joy and purpose in worship, family, community service, and personal development.

- This detachment from materialism helps reduce stress, envy, and competition, allowing individuals to lead simpler, more satisfying lives. When one's happiness is not dependent on accumulating wealth or status, they are free to focus on the more profound aspects of life, such as their relationship with Allah, personal growth, and contributing to society.

Serving Humanity with Compassion:

- *Zuhd* emphasizes that wealth and resources are means, not ends. By detaching from the desire for accumulation, believers are more inclined to serve humanity selflessly. *zuhd* encourages a spirit of compassion, reminding Muslims that their true wealth lies in giving and helping others.

- Service to others is a powerful way to find purpose in life. By using their resources, time, and talents to improve the lives of others, Muslims embody the compassion and selflessness that Islam advocates. In this way, *zuhd* helps believers fulfill their purpose as stewards of Allah's creation.

4.6 The Balance of Zuhd and Engagement with the World

While *zuhd* calls for detachment from materialism, Islam encourages active engagement with the world to fulfill responsibilities, build a healthy society, and spread goodness. A balanced approach to *zuhd* allows Muslims to live productively in the world while remaining focused on the Hereafter.

Balancing Worldly Responsibilities and Spiritual Goals:

- Islam teaches believers to fulfill their worldly responsibilities, including work, family, and community service. The Quran advises, "But seek, with what Allah has given you, the Hereafter, and [yet], do not forget your share of the world" (Quran, AL-Qasas 28:77). This ayah highlights the importance of balancing material pursuits with spiritual goals.

- A balanced approach to *zuhd* encourages Muslims to view work, family, and community obligations as part of their worship, ensuring they contribute positively to society while staying spiritually grounded.

Fulfilling Obligations with Excellence (Ihsan):

- Ihsan, or striving for excellence, applies to all aspects of a believer's life. By practicing *zuhd* without neglecting responsibilities, Muslims demonstrate their commitment to fulfilling their duties with integrity and sincerity.

- A person who practices Ihsan does their best in their profession, family, and community, knowing that their actions are a form of worship when done for Allah's sake. *Zuhd* does not mean lowering one's standards; rather, it means engaging with the world without becoming attached.

Detachment as a Path to True Freedom:

- Ultimately, *zuhd* frees believers from the anxieties and pressures of the *dunya*. By detaching from excessive desires, they gain the freedom to live authentically and prioritize what truly matters. This inner freedom allows Muslims to focus on worship, service, and spiritual growth without the distractions of worldly attachments.

- This freedom fosters resilience, empowering believers to navigate life's challenges with confidence and a sense of purpose. When one's heart is detached from the *dunya*, it becomes easier to trust Allah, stay content, and pursue a path that leads to lasting fulfillment.

Conclusion

Zuhd, or indifference to the dunya, is a principle that fosters spiritual strength, contentment, and purpose. By detaching from worldly attachments, Muslims open their hearts to a life centered on Allah, inner peace, and service to humanity. In an age marked by materialism, *zuhd* offers a refreshing perspective, encouraging believers to seek fulfillment in faith, personal integrity, and compassion.

Practicing *zuhd* is a lifelong journey of learning to live in the world without being consumed by it, engaging fully in one's responsibilities while keeping the heart focused on Allah. This balance of worldly engagement and spiritual detachment is key to living a life of true purpose, preparing for the eternal Hereafter, and embodying the beautiful teachings of Islam. Through *zuhd*, Muslims are reminded that their ultimate destination lies with Allah, and that every step taken with detachment, gratitude, and sincerity brings them closer to this goal.

CHAPTER FIVE

Achieving Spiritual and Communal Balance

I slam emphasizes a balanced approach to life, encouraging believers to fulfill their spiritual obligations to Allah and their responsibilities to their families, communities, and society. This balanced approach is a recurring theme in the Quran and Hadith, as well as in the teachings of classical scholars. Achieving harmony between personal spirituality and community engagement is essential for a fulfilling life in Islam. This chapter explores the importance of spiritual renewal, finding purpose in daily life, handling personal and organizational failures, and supporting each other's spiritual growth.

5.1 Spiritual Renewal and Rejuvenation

Spiritual renewal, or revitalizing one's connection with Allah, is a continual process in Islam. It involves revisiting and strengthening one's faith, re-engaging with religious practices, and reflecting on one's relationship with the Creator. In Islam, the heart and soul require regular nourishment and care, just as the body does. Without conscious efforts to renew spirituality, individuals may be drifting from their purpose and feel disconnected from their faith.

The Need for Spiritual Renewal:

- Life's demands, struggles, and distractions can drain one's spirituality. People may become so absorbed in their day-to-day responsibilities and ambitions that they unintentionally neglect their connection with Allah. Recognizing the need for spiritual renewal is the first step toward maintaining a fulfilling relationship with Allah.

- Imam al-Haddad's *Book of Assistance* emphasizes the importance of dedicating time to self-reflection, repentance, and acts of worship that nourish the soul. According to Imam al-Haddad, consistent renewal is essential to combat spiritual weariness, reinvigorate one's purpose, and focus on Allah.

Methods of Spiritual Renewal:

- **Daily *Dhikr* (Remembrance of Allah)**: *Dhikr*, or the remembrance of Allah, plays a central role in revitalizing spirituality. Simple phrases like "SubhanAllah" (Glory be to Allah), "Alhamdulillah" (All praise is due to Allah), and "Allahu Akbar" (Allah is the Greatest) bring peace to the heart and draw one closer to Allah. Dhikr cultivates mindfulness and keeps the heart engaged with the Creator throughout the day.

- **Prayer and Supplication (Du'a)**: Regular prayer (Salah) and supplication (Du'a) serve as lifelines that renew one's commitment to Allah. By setting aside time to pray sincerely and make dua, believers reconnect with their faith and reinforce their reliance on Allah. The Prophet Muhammad (peace and blessings be upon him) said, "The closest a servant comes to his Lord is when he is in prostration," emphasizing the powerful connection established during prayer.

- **Seeking Knowledge**: Pursuing beneficial knowledge strengthens faith and enhances one's understanding of Islam. Learning about the Quran, Hadith, and the lives of righteous figures offers new perspectives, motivates self-improvement, and inspires one's journey of spiritual growth.

Periodic Retreats and Isolation (Khalwa):

- *Khalwa*, or spiritual retreat, is a practice embraced by many classical scholars. Taking time away from the distractions of daily life to focus solely on worship, reflection, and dhikr can help purify the heart and provide clarity. Even if it's for a few hours or days, moments of seclusion allow individuals to reconnect with Allah and renew their intentions.

Reflection and Gratitude:

- Reflection (*muraqabah*) on Allah's blessings, as well as expressing gratitude, brings believers closer to Him. By recognizing and thanking Allah for all that He has provided, believers strengthen their faith and cultivate a positive outlook. This gratitude creates a sense of contentment and reinforces reliance on Allah, helping them maintain a balanced, purpose-driven life.

5.2 Purpose in Everyday Life

Islam teaches that a believer's purpose should permeate every aspect of life, from professional duties to personal interactions. This purpose begins with setting the right intention, or *niyyah*, for each action. By ensuring that their intentions align with Allah's pleasure, Muslims can transform daily tasks into acts of worship, thus achieving a life that is spiritually fulfilling and socially responsible.

The Role of Niyyah (Intention):

- The Prophet Muhammad (peace and blessings be upon him) said, "Actions are judged by intentions, and every person will get what they intended." This hadith emphasizes that the value of any action depends on the underlying intention. Whether it's work, study, or family care, if done with the intention of seeking Allah's pleasure, these acts become part of one's worship.

- By setting a sincere intention before any task, believers can infuse their lives with purpose, transforming mundane actions into meaningful deeds. This approach bridges the gap between spiritual and worldly activities, creating a life where every action serves a greater purpose.

Finding Purpose in Work and Family Responsibilities:

- **Work as Worship**: Islam views earning a lawful income as an act of worship when done with integrity and intention. Supporting one's family, helping others, and contributing positively to society are ways in which work becomes a reflection of one's faith. The Prophet (peace and blessings be upon him) said, "The best of earnings are from a man's own hand" (Ahmad & Nasa'i), highlighting the dignity and value of honest work.

- **Family as a Source of Barakah (Blessing)**: Islam places a high value on family life, viewing it as a means of spiritual and moral development. By fulfilling responsibilities to family members with kindness, patience, and generosity, one fulfills part of their duty to Allah. For instance, caring for one's parents is considered a path to paradise, as demonstrated in the Prophet's hadith, "Paradise lies at the feet of mothers" (Nasa'i & Ahmad). When nurtured with love and faith, family life becomes a source of blessings and a means of drawing closer to Allah.

Acts of Kindness and Charity:

- Purpose in Islam is not limited to personal actions but extends to benefiting others. Small acts of kindness, such as helping a neighbor, giving charity, or offering a kind word, have significant spiritual value. The Prophet Muhammad (peace and blessings be upon him) said, "Even a smile is charity" (Sunan At-Tirmidhi). By prioritizing kindness daily, believers can embody the compassionate spirit of Islam and serve as positive examples for others.

Personal Goals and Self-Improvement:

- Striving for self-improvement is a key aspect of purposeful living. Islam encourages believers to continuously improve themselves, whether by learning new skills, developing positive habits, or overcoming personal weaknesses. Setting realistic, meaningful goals in areas like health, education, and spirituality allows Muslims to grow and fulfill their potential in a balanced way.

5.3 Handling Personal and Organizational Failures

Failure is a natural part of life, and Islam provides guidance on how to deal with setbacks in a constructive manner. Personal failures, such as not meeting spiritual goals, and organizational challenges, like mismanagement within Islamic institutions, can be sources of frustration and disappointment. However, Islam teaches that failures are opportunities for growth, patience, and self-reflection, providing valuable lessons that strengthen a believer's character.

Learning from Personal Failures:

- **Recognizing and Acknowledging Mistakes**: Islam encourages believers to reflect on their mistakes and seek Allah's forgiveness. The Prophet Muhammad (peace and blessings be upon him) said, "All the children of Adam are sinners, and the best of sinners are those who repent" (Ibn Majah & Jami' At-Tirmidhi). Acknowledging errors with humility and repenting sincerely is the first step toward self-improvement.

- **Embracing Patience and Perseverance**: Personal failures can be emotionally challenging, but they also offer a chance to develop patience (*sabr*) and resilience. Allah says, "Indeed, Allah is with the patient" (Quran, Al-Baqarah 2:153). By enduring setbacks with patience and trusting in Allah's wisdom, believers learn to view failure as a temporary setback that ultimately brings them closer to their purpose.

Organizational Failures and Community Challenges:

- **Recognizing Common Challenges in Islamic Institutions**: Mosques and Islamic organizations often face challenges related to leadership, financial constraints, and internal conflicts. These issues can hinder their ability to serve the community effectively and may lead to feelings of disillusionment among members.

- **Adopting a Collaborative Approach to Problem-Solving**: When faced with organizational failures, community members must work together, communicate openly, and seek solutions that benefit everyone. By fostering a collaborative atmosphere, Islamic institutions can overcome challenges, strengthen their mission, and serve as models of resilience for the community.

Seeking Growth and Positive Change:

- **Commitment to Self-Improvement**: Every failure is an opportunity for growth. Instead of being discouraged, both individuals and organizations should assess their weaknesses, set goals for improvement, and work toward better outcomes. Continuous improvement is a lifelong process in Islam, helping believers and communities reach their potential.

- **Focusing on Allah's Wisdom**: Believers are encouraged to remember that Allah's wisdom often lies beyond human understanding. Difficulties and setbacks are part of His divine plan, intended to test, strengthen, and guide believers. By focusing on this perspective, individuals and organizations can find meaning and purpose even in their challenges.

5.4 Supporting Each Other's Spiritual Growth

Islamic teachings emphasize the importance of mutual support and guidance in building a strong, faith-centered community. When individuals support one another's spiritual growth, they contribute to a positive environment that fosters resilience, compassion, and shared values. This mutual support is integral to maintaining a balanced community where each member feels valued and connected to their faith.

Encouraging Good Deeds and Positive Habits:

- Islam encourages believers to support one another in righteousness and piety. The Quran states, "Help one another in righteousness and piety, but do not help one another in sin and transgression" (Quran, Al-Ma'ida 5:2). By motivating each other to perform good deeds, uphold honesty, and strive for self-improvement, community members create a positive, faith-driven environment that uplifts everyone.

- Simple acts, like encouraging a friend to pray, reminding each other to give charity, or inviting others to religious gatherings, can reinforce positive habits and help individuals stay connected to their faith.

Providing Emotional and Spiritual Support:

- Life's challenges can be overwhelming, and having a supportive community makes a significant difference. Islamic teachings emphasize empathy and kindness, encouraging believers to support one another in times of difficulty. The Prophet Muhammad (peace and blessings be upon him) said, "The believers in their mutual kindness, compassion, and sympathy are just like one body. When one limb suffers, the whole body responds with wakefulness and fever" (Bukhari & Muslim).

- Emotional support, such as lending a listening ear or offering words of encouragement, can help individuals navigate personal struggles. Spiritual support, like praying for each other's well-being or offering guidance based on Islamic teachings, fosters a sense of unity and compassion within the community.

Fostering Accountability Through Friendship:

- Friendships based on shared values play a powerful role in supporting spiritual growth. Islam encourages believers to choose friends who inspire them to be better and hold them accountable to their faith. The Prophet Muhammad (peace and blessings be upon him) said, "A person is upon the religion of their close friend, so be careful whom you befriend" (Abu Dawood & Jami' At-Tirmidhi).

- By choosing friends who remind each other of Allah, believers create a network of accountability that helps them stay committed to their spiritual goals. These friendships provide a source of motivation and accountability, encouraging each person to uphold Islamic values in their daily lives.

Organizing Community Initiatives for Collective Growth:

- Islamic centers and community organizations can play a vital role in supporting collective spiritual growth. Programs such as Quran study groups, weekly halaqas (religious circles), charity drives, and volunteer opportunities create a structured environment for community engagement and mutual support.

- These initiatives not only strengthen individual faith but also promote a sense of unity and shared purpose. By participating in such activities, community members actively contribute to an environment where each person's spiritual and communal well-being is nurtured.

5.5 Building a Future with Purpose

A balanced life that fulfills both spiritual and communal obligations is a life that reflects the essence of Islam. By committing to personal growth, supporting one another, and contributing to society, Muslims can live purposefully and create a lasting, positive impact on the world around them.

The Power of Consistent Effort:

- Islam teaches that small, consistent actions are the most beloved to Allah. The Prophet Muhammad (peace and blessings be upon him) said, "The best deeds are those done regularly, even if they are few" (Bukhari & Muslim). By incorporating consistent spiritual practices, acts of service, and moments of self-reflection, believers can achieve lasting spiritual growth and maintain a balanced life.

Striving for Both Spiritual and Societal Betterment:

- A balanced life is one that fulfills both personal and societal responsibilities. Islam encourages believers to serve Allah by serving humanity, striving to be sources of goodness and benefit to those around them. By engaging in charitable acts, supporting community initiatives, and upholding justice, Muslims demonstrate their commitment to a life of purpose.

- This dual focus ensures that individuals not only grow spiritually but also contribute positively to society, fulfilling their roles as ambassadors of Islam.

Continuing the Legacy of the Prophet Muhammad (peace and blessings be upon him):

- The Prophet Muhammad's (peace and blessings be upon him) life exemplifies a balance between devotion to Allah and service to others. He fulfilled his spiritual duties with dedication and showed compassion, kindness, and generosity toward all people. Following his example allows Muslims to find harmony in their lives, serving as models of balanced living for future generations.

Conclusion

Achieving spiritual and communal balance is a lifelong journey in Islam, one that requires commitment, self-reflection, and mutual support. By nurturing one's relationship with Allah, setting purposeful intentions, learning from failures, and supporting others, Muslims can lead lives of meaning, resilience, and compassion. This balance allows believers to embody the values of Islam in every facet of life, creating a positive, faith-centered community that reflects the beauty and wisdom of Islamic teachings. Through this harmonious approach, Muslims fulfill their ultimate purpose: to serve Allah by uplifting themselves and those around them.

CHAPTER SIX

Personal Cleanliness, Dress, and Appearance

P ersonal cleanliness, attire, and appearance are not merely acts of hygiene or style but essential elements of faith, reflecting one's inner state and obedience to Allah. They embody gratitude, humility, and respect for oneself and others, honoring the natural disposition (*fitra*) that Allah has bestowed upon humankind.

6.1 Personal Cleanliness

- **Inward Cleanliness**
  Inward cleanliness involves purifying the soul from harmful traits such as pride, ostentation, envy, and excessive attachment to worldly desires. Instead, one should cultivate virtues like humility, modesty, sincerity, and generosity. True inward purity is achieved by consistently replacing negative attributes with noble ones, aligning one's character with the values of the Quran and Sunnah.

- **Outward Cleanliness**
  Outward cleanliness encompasses avoiding sinful acts and remaining steadfast in obedience. A person achieves complete outward cleanliness when they consistently engage in good deeds and exhibit praiseworthy behavior, both in public and private. However, the degree of cleanliness corresponds to how far one distances oneself from blameworthy traits and behaviors while embracing positive ones.

- **Wudu' (Ablution)**
  Renew your *wudu'* before each obligatory prayer and strive to remain in a state of ritual purity as much as possible. Make wudu' again whenever it is invalidated, as it serves as a spiritual shield for the believer. It is said that *wudu'* is the weapon of the believer, and when armed with it, enemies dare not approach. After performing *wudu'*, pray two rak'ahs as an act of devotion. If you cannot always maintain *wudu'*, aim to do so during specific acts of worship, such as sitting in the mosque, reciting the Quran, seeking knowledge, engaging in dhikr, or performing other forms of devotion.

- **Ghusl (Full Purification)**
  Perform *ghusl* regularly with the intention of maintaining personal cleanliness, even when not in a state of major ritual impurity (*junub*). The Sunnah recommends performing *ghusl* on Fridays for those attending the Friday prayer, as it embodies both physical and spiritual purification.

- **Supplication After Wudu' or Ghusl**
  When you complete *wudu'* or *ghusl*, say:
  "Ash-hadu an la ilaha illa'llahu la sharika lahu, wa ash-hadu anna Muhammadan 'abduhu wa rasuluh"
  ("I testify that there is no deity but Allah alone, without partners, and I testify that Muhammad is His servant and Messenger").
  This supplication, taken from the teachings of Imam al-Haddad, reinforces one's commitment to faith and devotion.

- **Significance of Personal Grooming and Cleanliness**
  Personal hygiene is foundational to Islamic teachings. The Prophet Muhammad (peace and blessings be upon him) emphasized, "Five practices are part of the natural disposition (*fitra*): circumcision, removing pubic hair, plucking armpit hair, trimming the mustache, and clipping the nails" (Bukhari & Muslim). These practices, recommended for all believers, are about cleanliness and honoring one's natural state.

- **Grooming Practices of the Fitra**
  The Prophet (peace and blessings be upon him) further highlighted that actions like rinsing the mouth and nose, using a toothstick (*siwak*), and cleaning oneself after using the restroom are acts that maintain the believer's purity and health.

- **Circumcision and Hair Removal**
  Circumcision is a recommended practice for males, symbolizing purity. Similarly, removing pubic and armpit hair is encouraged to maintain cleanliness, ideally once a week, with a maximum period of forty days. Men are traditionally advised to shave and women to pluck, though both methods are permissible for fulfilling the sunnah.

- **Trimming the Moustache and Growing the Beard**
  Men are encouraged to keep their mustaches trimmed so they do not cover the upper lip and to grow a beard, reflecting a dignified appearance. However, any beard longer than a fist's length may be trimmed following the sunnah.

- **Clipping Nails and Toothstick (Siwak)**
  Clipping nails weekly ensures hygiene and adherence to the sunnah, while using a toothstick cleanses the mouth and pleases Allah; as the Prophet (peace and blessings be upon him) stated, "The toothstick purifies the mouth and pleases the Lord" (Bukhari & Nasa'i).

- **Cleanliness After Using the Toilet (Istinja)**
  Islam strongly emphasizes cleanliness after relieving oneself, known as *istinja*. This practice involves thorough cleansing, reinforcing the importance of hygiene and purity before approaching acts of worship.

- **Bathing and Disposal of Hair and Nails**
  Regular bathing is encouraged, with at least one bath recommended weekly. Furthermore, hair and nails should be respectfully disposed of, ideally by burial, as a sign of respect for one's physical self.

6.2 Personal Appearance

- **Guiding Principles of Appearance and Clothing**
  Islamic principles of appearance are rooted in gratitude, humility, and contentment. Presenting oneself well is a form of gratitude for Allah's blessings, while maintaining humility acknowledges that beauty and resources are blessings from Allah. Unnecessary alterations to appearance, out of vanity or dissatisfaction with one's features, are discouraged as they may reflect discontent with Allah's creation.

- **Hair Care and Grooming**
  The Prophet (peace and blessings be upon him) advised, "Whoever has hair, let him care for it." Regular washing, oiling, and combing keep the hair neat and healthy. Men may groom their hair or shave their heads, while women are encouraged to maintain long hair to avoid resembling men.

- **Facial Hair Management**
  Women can remove facial hair to beautify themselves, especially for their spouses. Men may manage their eyebrows and other facial hair within the limits of modesty, avoiding any style that imitates feminine fashion.

- **Permissible and Impermissible Hair Alterations**
  While adding human hair to one's own is forbidden, using animal hair for cosmetic purposes is permissible. Dyeing white hair in colors other than black is recommended, especially with *ithmid* kohl, which also benefits eyesight.

- **Use of Mirrors and Perfume**
  The Prophet (peace and blessings be upon him) would look in the mirror and recite, "All praise is for Allah who fashioned my form and made it balanced" (Ahmad & Adab al-Mufrad). Perfume is a recommended practice. Men are encouraged to wear noticeable scents, while women should use subtle fragrances when in public to uphold modesty.

6.3 Dress and Clothing

- **Rules on Clothing**
  Modesty in clothing is obligatory. Men must cover from the navel to the knees, and women must cover all but the face, hands, and feet when among non-mahram. The intention behind dressing well is crucial; wearing quality attire is permissible as long as it reflects gratitude without pride or excess.

- **Maintaining Modesty and Avoiding Arrogance**
  Clothing should not be worn out of pride, and men are specifically warned against garments that drag below the ankles. Islamic dress encourages moderation, neither too extravagant nor excessively poor, reflecting dignity and respect.

- **Impermissible Practices in Dress**
  Islam forbids tight or transparent clothing that reveals the private areas (*awrah*), clothing that imitates the opposite gender, and adopting distinctive non-Muslim fashions without reason. Such guidelines preserve the Muslim's identity, modesty, and adherence to faith.

- **Silk and Jewelry**
  Men are prohibited from wearing pure silk or gold as adornment, though silver rings under 5 grams are permissible, often worn on the little finger of the left hand. Women are permitted to wear all forms of jewelry and may even use gold for medical purposes if needed. "Gold and silk have been permitted for the females of my Ummah and prohibited for the males." (Sunan An-Nasa'i)

In summary, personal cleanliness, dress, and appearance in Islam are acts of worship rooted in faith and acknowledging Allah's blessings. By adhering to these practices, Muslims cultivate gratitude, humility, and modesty, fostering both physical cleanliness and spiritual growth. These actions not only enhance one's connection with Allah but also contribute to a dignified and respectful presence within the community.

CHAPTER SEVEN

Earning a Living

In Islam, earning a living is more than a means to material wealth; it is a purposeful pursuit aligned with faith, ethics, and social responsibility. Through honest work, Muslims demonstrate reliance on Allah, fulfill their responsibilities, and contribute positively to society. The Prophet Muhammad (peace be upon him) and other prophets exemplified a balanced approach to work, one rooted in the values of sincerity, integrity, and humility.

7.1 Foundations of Earning a Living

- **Reliance on Allah**
  A Muslim believes that sustenance ultimately comes from Allah. This understanding fosters honesty and integrity, as no amount of deceit can change what Allah has decreed. The Prophet Muhammad (peace and blessings be upon him) said, "If you were to rely on Allah as He should be relied upon, He would provide for you as He provides for the birds; they leave their nests hungry and return full" (At-Tirmidhi & Ibn Majah). This reliance encourages honest work, knowing that Allah is the ultimate Provider.

- **Utilizing Available Means**
  While sustenance is from Allah, Islam encourages believers to use the means Allah has provided. Effort is seen as an act of obedience, yet the outcome is left to Allah's will. This perspective helps one remain productive without becoming overly attached to the results of their work.

- **Fulfilling Responsibilities**
  Islam emphasizes that individuals are accountable for providing for themselves and their dependents. The Prophet Muhammad (peace and blessings be upon him) warned, "It is a sufficient sin for a man to neglect those he is responsible for." (Abu Dawud & Ahmad). By meeting their family's needs, Muslims fulfill an important religious duty.

- **Seeking Pure and Lawful Income**
  Purity in income is essential in Islam. The Prophet (peace and blessings be upon him) stated, "Any flesh nourished by unlawful means will not enter Paradise; the Fire is more suited for it."(Ahmad & Sunan al-Kubra al-Bayhaqi). Lawful income not only sustains the body but also brings blessings, facilitates answered prayers, and strengthens one's spiritual connection to Allah.

- **Earning with Noble Intentions**
  The Prophet Muhammad (peace and blessings be upon him) praised those who earn to avoid dependency, support family, and help the community, saying they would meet Allah with a radiant face. Conversely, those who seek wealth solely for pride or vanity may face His displeasure. This underscores the importance of intention in every aspect of earning a livelihood.

7.2 Categories and Ethics of Earning

- **Categories of Earning**

  - **Obligatory**: Every Muslim must earn enough to cover their basic needs and those of their dependents.

  - **Recommended**: Earning beyond basic needs is encouraged if the surplus is used to support relatives, assist the needy, or benefit society.

  - **Permissible**: Seeking additional comfort or adornment through work is allowed, provided it does not lead to arrogance or extravagance.

  - **Prohibited**: Earning solely for boasting or pride—even if lawful—is discouraged, as it reflects a misaligned purpose.

- **Restrictions on Begging**
  Islam generally discourages begging unless one cannot meet one's essential needs. The dignity in work, even humble work, is emphasized, as self-sufficiency is highly valued.

- **Prophetic Example of Work**
  Working for one's sustenance aligns with the practices of the prophets. Prophet Dawud (peace be upon him) earned through making armor, and Prophet Muhammad (peace and blessings be upon him) tended sheep. Their example highlights that no work, when honest and lawful, is undignified.

- **Benefits of Employment**
  Working fosters discipline, resilience, and self-respect. It also reduces dependency on others, contributes to society, and allows for the healthy utilization of one's time and skills.

7.3 Etiquette in Earning a Living

- **Setting the Right Intentions**
  Working with the intention of fulfilling responsibilities, supporting loved ones, and contributing to society elevates the act of earning to a form of worship. Seeking to avoid dependency on others is a noble pursuit in Islam.

- **Starting the Day Early**
  The Prophet (peace be upon him) prayed for blessings upon those who begin their day's work early. This practice reflects the wisdom of making the most of one's time and benefiting from the day's early hours.

- **Balancing Work and Worship**
  Islam encourages productivity without neglecting one's religious obligations. Believers should ensure that work does not prevent them from fulfilling duties to Allah, such as prayer and other acts of worship.

- **Moderation in Seeking Wealth**
  Wealth should be pursued ethically, without allowing it to overshadow one's principles. The Prophet (peace be upon him) advised, "Seek your provision in a beautiful manner: take the lawful and leave the unlawful." (Musnad al-Bazzar, Hadith 8943; Shu'ab al-Iman, Hadith 5812). This

guidance encourages Muslims to remain mindful of ethical boundaries.

- **Business Etiquette**
  Muslims are encouraged to uphold honesty and fairness in all business dealings. This includes avoiding excessive greed, maintaining transparency, allowing fair prices, avoiding deceit, and honoring returns if a buyer regrets a purchase. Islam stresses that profits should not come at the expense of ethics.

7.4 Illicit Gains and Ethical Scrupulousness

- **Avoiding Illicit Earnings**
  Income from bribery, usury, or other unethical means is prohibited. Pure and lawful earnings benefit both the individual and society, while unethical gains bring spiritual harm and mistrust within the community.

- **Maintaining Ethical Standards**
  Islam encourages caution around income sources that are questionable or ethically ambiguous. The Prophet (peace be upon him) said that a person who avoids doubtful matters will earn the approval of Allah.

- **Purifying Wealth**
  If wealth is earned through impermissible means, it should be given away for public welfare, without seeking reward, as Allah accepts only sincere intentions in charity.

- **Examples of Prohibited Earnings**

  - **Bribery**: Influencing decisions through bribes is forbidden.

  - **Deception**: Pretending to be needy or righteous to receive financial aid is dishonest and haram.

  - **Coerced Earnings**: Accepting money from others through pressure or shame is impermissible.

- **Ethical Transactions**
  Islam forbids earning through means that support sinful actions, such as supplying items that are known to facilitate sin. Usurious transactions (interest-based earnings) are also impermissible, and accepting gifts from

those with unethical income is discouraged unless the gift is clearly traceable to lawful sources.

Conclusion

Earning a living in Islam is a purposeful journey rooted in reliance on Allah, ethical conduct, and responsibility toward oneself and society. By approaching work with sincerity, honesty, and gratitude, Muslims align with Prophetic teachings and foster a balanced life that meets worldly needs while honoring spiritual values. Through their labor, they reflect the principles of living Islam with purpose—maintaining a livelihood that not only sustains the body but nourishes the soul.

CHAPTER EIGHT

The Etiquette and Significance of Eating and Drinking

I slamic teachings place great importance on the etiquettes of eating and drinking, as these daily acts provide believers with opportunities to reflect gratitude, self-discipline, and mindfulness toward Allah. The way we consume food and drink embodies Islamic values, reminding us to be grateful for Allah's blessings and to use our sustenance to strengthen our physical and spiritual well-being.

8.1 Principles of Eating and Drinking in Islam

- **Gratitude**
  The act of eating is one of the most evident blessings from Allah, and gratitude for this blessing is integral to Islamic practice. This gratitude is expressed by respecting food, avoiding waste, and using the energy from our food to worship and serve Allah. Sitting with humility and saying "Alhamdulillah" (All praise is for Allah) before and after eating demonstrates an awareness of the gift we have been given.

- **Moderation and Purpose**
  Eating with purpose, rather than indulgence, aligns with the Islamic principle of moderation. A Muslim eats to live, not to overindulge and aims to consume food mindfully to stay healthy and able to fulfill their religious obligations. The Prophet Muhammad (peace and blessings be upon him) advised believers to eat moderately: "The son of Adam does

not fill any vessel worse than his stomach. It is sufficient for him to eat a few mouthfuls to sustain him. But if he must (fill it), then a third for his food, a third for his drink, and a third for his breath." (Sunan Ibn Majah, Hadith 3349; Musnad Ahmad, 17186)

8.2 Categories of Eating

Islamic teachings categorize eating based on purpose and necessity:

- **Obligatory**: Consuming enough to maintain health and fulfill obligations, such as standing in prayer.

- **Recommended**: Eating slightly more to gain strength for additional acts of worship and studying knowledge.

- **Permissible**: Eating to fullness if it increases physical and mental energy.

- **Disliked**: Eating beyond fullness without a specific purpose.

- **Forbidden**: Overeating to the point of indulgence or wastefulness unless there is a valid reason, such as fasting preparation or ensuring a guest feels comfortable.

8.3 Recommended Practices While Eating

The Prophet Muhammad (peace be upon him) provided comprehensive guidelines for eating with dignity, humility, and purpose. Here are key etiquettes encouraged in Islam:

- **Begin with Intention**
  Before eating, set the intention to use the meal's energy to serve Allah. Refrain from eating unless genuinely hungry, and stop before reaching complete fullness.

- **Humility and Sitting on the Ground**
  The Prophet (peace and blessings be upon him) would eat humbly, often on the ground, saying, "I eat as a slave eats. I sit as a slave sits. I am but a slave." (Sunan Abu Dawood, 2855). Sitting on a mat or on the ground reflects humility and enhances gratitude.

- **Sharing Meals**
  Eating together brings blessings, promotes unity, and fosters gratitude. The Prophet (peace and blessings be upon him) said, "The best food is that over which many hands reach." He also encouraged eating in groups as it increases blessings in the food.

- **Saying "Bismillah"**
  Begin every meal by saying "Bismillah" (In the name of Allah) to invite blessings and protect the meal from harmful effects. If forgotten, one should say "Bismillah awwalahu wa aakhirahu" (In the name of Allah, in its beginning and its end) upon remembering. The Prophet Muhammad (peace and blessings be upon him) said: "Indeed, Allah is pleased with a servant who eats a morsel (of food) and praises Him for it, or drinks a sip (of water) and praises Him for it." (Sahih Muslim, 2734)

- **Expressing Gratitude at the End**
  Saying "Alhamdulillah" (All praise is for Allah) at the end of the meal shows thanks for Allah's provision. The Prophet (peace and blessings be upon him) taught, "Whoever says, 'All praise is for Allah who fed me this and provided it to me without any ability of mine or power,' his previous sins are forgiven." (Jami' at-Tirmidhi, Hadith 3458; Sunan Ibn Majah, 3285)

- **Eating with the Right Hand**
  The Prophet (peace be upon him) instructed that one should eat and drink with the right hand, as it represents good habits and is in contrast to the practices of shaytan. The Prophet Muhammad (peace and blessings be upon him) said: "When one of you eats, let him eat with his right hand, and when he drinks, let him drink with his right hand, for the devil eats with his left hand and drinks with his left hand." (Sahih Muslim, 2020).

- **Avoiding Waste**
  Every morsel is a blessing; thus, food should not be wasted. Picking up and eating even the smallest crumbs reflects veneration for Allah's blessings. The Prophet Muhammad (peace and blessings be upon him) said: "When one of you eats, let him not wipe his hand until he has licked it or had it licked, for he does not know in which part of the food the blessing lies." (Sahih Muslim, Hadith 2033; Sahih al-Bukhari, 5456)

* **Respecting Bread**
Bread holds special reverence, as a staple and essential food source. Showing respect includes picking up fallen pieces, refraining from discarding them carelessly, and ensuring it is shared rather than wasted. The Prophet Muhammad (peace and blessings be upon him) said: "Honor bread, for Allah has sent blessings upon it." (Mustadrak al-Hakim, Hadith 7132; Shu'ab al-Iman, 5522)

8.4 Guidelines for Drinking

Islamic etiquette extends to drinking, where similar mindfulness and gratitude are encouraged:

* **Hold the Cup in the Right Hand**
Start with "Bismillah" and end with "Alhamdulillah," acknowledging Allah's gift of sustenance and health.

* **Drink in Sips**
Drink slowly and in three breaths, rather than large gulps, to reflect calmness and appreciation for each sip. The Prophet (peace be upon him) discouraged drinking in a single gulp or while breathing over the cup, which respects both the blessing of water and the communal setting.

* **Accepting Zamzam Water**
Zamzam water holds a unique spiritual significance, and it is considered blessed, so it is encouraged to accept it when offered.

* **Drinking While Sitting**
Sitting while drinking is preferred as it promotes calmness and humility, although drinking while standing is permissible for specific cases like drinking Zamzam water.

* **Avoid Waste and Show Gratitude**
As with food, it is important not to waste water, respecting it as a source of life and a gift from Allah.

8.5 Lawful and Unlawful Foods

Islamic teachings provide specific guidelines on permissible and impermissible foods intended to preserve both physical and spiritual health:

- **Lawful (Halal) Foods**
  Halal foods include most plant-based foods, fish, and animals that have been slaughtered according to Islamic guidelines by a Muslim, Jew, or Christian while mentioning Allah's name.

- **Unlawful (Haram) Foods**
  Forbidden foods include predatory animals, pigs, and improperly slaughtered animals. Islam also prohibits consuming harmful substances such as poison, dirt, and foods that may cause health issues.

- **Intoxicating Substances**
  All intoxicating substances, including alcohol, are strictly forbidden as they impair judgment and disrupt the clarity and mindfulness that Islam promotes.

8.6 The Spiritual Aspect of Food and Drink

- **Food as a Means of Spiritual Growth**
  Eating in accordance with Islamic guidelines strengthens faith, enhances gratitude, and serves as a reminder of Allah's blessings. By mindfully eating and drinking with gratitude and humility, Muslims can transform these daily actions into acts of worship.

- **Preparing for the Hereafter**
  Recognizing food as a blessing also reminds us that it is temporary, meant to sustain us in our journey toward the Hereafter. By eating with purpose, moderation, and intention, Muslims honor the role of food in their lives as a tool for worship rather than indulgence.

Conclusion: Eating and Drinking as Acts of Worship

Islamic etiquette for eating and drinking encompasses both physical and spiritual dimensions. By observing these etiquettes, Muslims turn mundane actions into expressions of faith, gratitude, and mindfulness, aligning themselves with moderation and humility. Every meal offers an opportunity to draw closer to Allah, use His blessings for righteous purposes, and remember the true purpose of life. Through gratitude, mindful consumption, and lawful choices, believers can honor their sustenance as a means of worship and a bridge toward Allah's favor.

CHAPTER NINE

Extravagance, Sports, and Pastimes

I slamic teachings encourage Muslims to lead lives of purpose and moderation, particularly regarding wealth, leisure, and recreational activities. By valuing time, honoring Allah's blessings, and setting boundaries around indulgence, Muslims can maintain balance and discipline in their daily lives. This chapter outlines the principles of living with intention, addressing wastefulness, recreational activities, and permissible forms of entertainment.

9.1 Purposeful Use of Time and Wealth

- **Honoring Allah's Blessings**
  Time, wealth, and health are blessings from Allah, meant to be used thoughtfully. The Prophet Muhammad (peace and blessings be upon him)said, "The feet of the servant will not move on the Day of Judgment until he is asked about four things: his life and how he spent it, his knowledge and how he acted upon it, his wealth—where he earned it and how he spent it, and his body and how he used it." (Sunan At-Tirmidhi, 2417). Every resource has a purpose, and spending it mindlessly dishonors this gift.

- **Focus on the Hereafter**
  The ultimate goal for Muslims is to live in this world with an eye on the Hereafter, using resources in ways that benefit both. The Qur'an reminds us, "By time, indeed, mankind is in loss" (Qur'an, Al-Asr 103:1-2), emphasizing that time, like other blessings, should be spent purposefully.

9.2 Avoiding Wastefulness (Israf)

Islam strongly discourages Israf, or wastefulness, which includes excessive spending on things that do not contribute to one's spiritual or worldly well-being. Wastefulness can erode gratitude and spiritual awareness, while thoughtful use of resources fosters a sense of responsibility.

- **Examples of Wastefulness**
  Wastefulness occurs not only through frivolous spending but also through neglect. Clear examples include letting food spoil, neglecting animals, or discarding items without considering their reuse or donation.

- **Subtle Forms of Wastefulness**
  Wastefulness can also take subtle forms, such as:

  ○ Neglecting food until it spoils,

  ○ Letting clothing or books deteriorate,

  ○ Overeating beyond one's need, or

  ○ Washing away food remnants instead of consuming them.

- **Extravagance in Lawful Things**
  Extravagance is allowed in permissible areas, like food, clothing, or hospitality, but it should be within reason and not lead to pride. Spending on special occasions to honor guests or celebrate achievements, for example, can be praiseworthy, as "there is no good in wastefulness, and no wastefulness in the good."

9.3 Use of Gold and Silver

Gold and silver represent wealth, and their use is carefully regulated in Islam. This ensures they are respected and not used excessively or frivolously.

- **Jewelry**
  Women may wear gold and silver jewelry without restriction. However, men are prohibited from wearing gold, though they may wear a silver ring.

- **Utensils and Household Items**
  Both men and women are forbidden from using utensils made of pure gold or silver, such as cups, plates, or pens. The Prophet (peace be upon him) said, "Whoever drinks from a vessel of gold or silver is filling his stomach with the fire of Hell." (Sahih Muslim, 2065; Sahih Bukhari, 5634). Using these materials for everyday items is seen as excessive and prideful, detracting from the value of humility.

- **Permissible Exceptions**
  It is permissible to use if gold or silver is merely an accessory (e.g., silver-tipped pens) or coated on an item without direct touch. However, if food or drink is served in a gold or silver container, it should be transferred to another vessel before consumption.

9.4 Sports and Leisure Activities

Recreational activities are permitted in Islam, but they should be in accordance with Islamic principles of purposefulness and moderation. Islam differentiates between productive activities that strengthen the body and mind and purposeless distractions.

- **Prohibited and Discouraged Games**
  Activities considered purely wasteful or purposeless (lahw) are discouraged. The Prophet (peace and blessings be upon him) said, "Every activity a Muslim man engages in is falsehood, except for shooting his bow, training his horse, or playing with his family. For these are from the truth" (Sunan At-Tirmidhi, 1637). Games involving gambling, immodesty, or those that promote neglect of responsibilities are also forbidden.

- **Lawful Games with Benefits**
  Sports and pastimes that strengthen the body, promote mental alertness, or encourage relaxation are encouraged, provided they are done in moderation and do not interfere with one's obligations. Examples include:

  - Archery, horseback riding, and swimming, which the Prophet (peace and blessings be upon him) explicitly recommended,

  - Games with family members, fostering bonds, and

○ Recreational activities that build health or skills without leading to overindulgence.

- **Competitions**
Competitions in sports or skills are allowed, provided they do not involve gambling or other prohibited elements. Acceptable prizes include those funded by a third party or non-participants.

9.5 Music and Entertainment

Entertainment is permitted with restrictions to ensure it aligns with Islamic values of modesty and mindfulness.

- **Permissible Forms of Singing**
Singing is allowed when it is free of immoral or suggestive lyrics. Songs that praise Allah express gratitude or have neutral content can be enjoyed as long as they do not distract from more important obligations.

- **Musical Instruments**
String and wind instruments, which are strongly associated with emotional indulgence, are generally discouraged. Simple percussion instruments, like the *duff*, are permitted, particularly during celebratory events like weddings and festivals.

9.6 Images and Illustrations

Islamic guidance on images seeks to avoid excessive attachment to depictions of living beings, as it may lead to idolatry or distraction from spiritual goals.

- **Creating Images**
Creating images or statues of living beings is discouraged. The Prophet (peace and blessings be upon him) said, "Those who make images will be punished on Judgment Day, and it will be said to them, 'Bring your creations to life!'" (Sahih Bukhari, 5951; Sahih Muslim, 2108). This restriction encourages focusing creativity on non-living elements or abstract forms.

- **Permissible Uses of Images**
Exceptions to this include:

○ Small images where facial details are not clear,

- ○ Pictures used in a non-dominant way, such as on household items or

- ○ Depictions that serve educational purposes and do not invite undue attention or pride.

Conclusion

Islam provides a balanced framework for approaching wealth, leisure, and recreation. By using resources wisely, avoiding waste, and selecting pastimes that benefit the body, mind, or relationships, Muslims can honor Allah's blessings and live with purpose. The Islamic approach to material and leisure activities is one of gratitude and moderation, where enjoying Allah's gifts aligns with humility and a focus on the Hereafter.

Mid Book Review Request

Dear Reader,

Thank you for joining me on this journey through *Living Islam with Purpose*. Your time, reflection, and commitment to deepening your faith mean so much. I hope these chapters have offered inspiration and practical insights to help you build a purposeful life rooted in Islamic values, both as an individual and as part of your community.

As you continue reflecting on the teachings and ideas within these pages, I would be sincerely grateful if you could share your thoughts with others. An honest review on Amazon, Goodreads, or your preferred platform would not only help others discover this book but also encourage more Muslims to embark on their own journey of living Islam with purpose. Your feedback is invaluable in spreading this message of faith, resilience, and meaningful living.

Please click the link or scan the QR code below to submit your review.

https://www.amazon.com/review/review-your-purchases/?asin=B0DNJ9Q CLS

Jazakum Allahu khairan – may your path be blessed and purposeful. Aameen.
Aisha Othman

CHAPTER TEN

Health, Sickness, and Death

Health, sickness, and death are intrinsic aspects of life, each offering unique opportunities for spiritual growth and reflection. Islam teaches that these experiences are not merely personal states but divine tests and blessings, guiding believers to strengthen their connection with Allah and refine their character. By embracing health as a gift, sickness as an opportunity for purification, and death as a reminder of our ultimate return to Allah, Muslims can navigate these stages of life with faith, resilience, and purpose.

10.1 Health: A Blessing and Responsibility

- **Health as a Blessing**
  Health is one of Allah's greatest blessings. The Prophet Muhammad (peace and blessings be upon him) said, "There are two blessings that many people are cheated out of: health and free time." (Sahih Bukhari, 6412). When we have both, it is vital to utilize them in obedience to Allah, recognizing that health enables us to fulfill our duties and engage in acts of worship. Ibn al-Jawzi said, "When health and free time are combined, and one still neglects good deeds, he is truly cheated."

- **Fear of Allah During Times of Health**
  A healthy person should maintain a sense of awe and fear of Allah, as health can sometimes lead to complacency. This sense of responsibility motivates one to use one's abilities to please Allah and avoid sin.

- **Gratitude and Usage of Health**
  Health should be used to strengthen one's connection with Allah, engage in worship, and contribute to the well-being of others. Failing to recognize the blessing of health is a form of ingratitude while using it for

harmful purposes shows a lack of respect for the gift bestowed by Allah.

10.2 Sickness: A Time of Patience and Purification

Islam regards sickness as a test, a form of purification, and an opportunity to draw closer to Allah. It provides a chance to reflect, repent, and rely solely on the mercy of Allah.

- **Embracing Sickness with Patience**
  The Prophet (peace and blessings be upon him) said, "No believer is afflicted with a thorn-prick or what is greater than that except that a higher degree is inscribed for him, or a sin is removed from him." (Sahih Bukhari, 5641; Sahih Muslim, 2572)

  Sickness, therefore, is not only a trial but a blessing in disguise, purifying sins and elevating ranks. Shaykh Abd al-Qadir al-Jilani taught that patience in sickness signals purification, while frustration may indicate punishment.

- **Avoiding Complaints**
  While expressing pain is permissible, a person should avoid excessive complaints that may reflect dissatisfaction with Allah's decree. The ideal approach is to say "Alhamdulillah" (All praise is for Allah) regardless of one's condition, recognizing it as a means of growing in faith and gratitude.

- **Seeking Treatment with Faith**
  The Prophet (peace and blessings be upon him) encouraged seeking medical treatment, saying, "Every ailment has a cure; if the cure meets the ailment, he is cured by Allah's permission." (Sahih Muslim, 2204; Sahih Bukhari, 5678). Medicine is an external means, but true healing lies in Allah's hands. If treatment is not available, relying on Allah's mercy is an expression of profound faith.

- **Avoiding Sins and Repentance**
  Sickness provides an opportunity to repent from past sins and adopt habits of remembrance, such as reciting specific supplications and the last three chapters of the Qur'an, as practiced by the Prophet's family.

10.3 Death: A Reminder of the Journey Back to Allah

Death, the inevitable return to our Creator, is a profound reminder of life's temporary nature and a transition to the Hereafter. Islam encourages believers to frequently remember death, not as a source of fear but as a motivator to lead a righteous life and fulfill obligations.

- **Remembering Death Regularly**
  The Prophet (peace and blessings be upon him) advised, "Remember often the terminator of pleasures." (Sunan Ibn Majah, 4258; Jami` at-Tirmidhi, 2307). This practice helps purify the heart, inspire contentment, and detach from worldly desires. Reflecting on death encourages one to live responsibly, seeing each day as a gift and opportunity to serve Allah.

- **Preparing for Death Without Fear**
  Islam teaches that a person should avoid desiring death solely due to worldly struggles. However, one may pray, "O Allah, give me life so long as life is better for me, and take my soul when death is better for me." This prayer shows acceptance of Allah's will.

- **Hope in Allah's Mercy at the End of Life**
  During the final stages of life, believers should place their hope in Allah's mercy, anticipating forgiveness and peace in the Hereafter. The Prophet (peace and blessings be upon him) said, "Let none of you die except having a good opinion of Allah." (Sahih Muslim, 2877). This optimistic outlook is crucial in the face of death, as it reflects trust in Allah's justice and compassion.

- **The Will and Bequests**
  A Muslim should prepare a will outlining any debts, unfulfilled religious obligations, and bequests. This not only fulfills the requirements of Islamic law but ensures that any missed prayers, fasting, or obligations can be compensated for, thus easing the soul's journey.

10.4 Facing Calamities: Strength Through Faith

- **The Sunnah of "Inna lillahi wa inna ilayhi raji'un"**
  When calamities occur, Muslims are encouraged to recite, "Verily we belong to Allah, and verily to Him do we return." (Quran, Al-Baqarah 2:156). This statement reminds believers that all matters return to Allah

and helps them find peace amid hardship.

- **Taking Inspiration from the Prophet's Tribulations**
  Reflecting on the trials faced by the Prophet Muhammad (peace and blessings be upon him) offers solace. The Prophet (peace and blessings be upon him) faced countless hardships, yet he remained patient and hopeful, a model of resilience and faith for his followers.

- **Finding Goodness in Every Condition**
  The Prophet (peace and blessings be upon him) said, "Wondrous is the affair of the believer, for there is good for him in every matter, and this is not the case with anyone except the believer: If he is happy, he thanks Allah, and it is good for him; and if he is harmed, he shows patience, and it is good for him." (Sahih Muslim, 2999).

Believers recognize every situation as a test of patience or gratitude, knowing that responding with faith transforms every condition into an opportunity for spiritual growth.

Conclusion: Embracing Health, Sickness, and Death with Faith and Purpose

Living Islam with purpose means facing life's natural phases—health, sickness, and death—with faith, resilience, and gratitude. Health should inspire one to serve Allah with vigor, while sickness invites patience and repentance. Death reminds us of our return to Allah, encouraging a life of righteousness and humility. Islam teaches that every condition is a chance to draw closer to Allah, transforming trials into means for spiritual elevation and ultimate success in the Hereafter.

CHAPTER ELEVEN

The Rights of Muslims

L iving as part of a community is essential in Islam, where the welfare of each individual is interconnected with the well-being of others. Islam encourages Muslims to foster relationships based on sincerity, kindness, respect, and compassion, helping build a society that reflects divine guidance and the best human character. This chapter explores the practical guidelines for fulfilling the rights of Muslims in daily interactions, nurturing a purposeful and supportive community.

11.1 Principles for Interacting with Fellow Muslims

In Islam, building relationships rooted in good character, empathy, and mutual respect is paramount. These values guide Muslims to foster an environment where love, support, and kindness flourish.

- **Exhibiting Good Character**
  Upholding excellent character is central to Islamic ethics. The Prophet Muhammad (peace and blessings be upon him) said, "The believer reaches the rank of the one who fasts and prays through good character." (Sunan Abu Dawud, 4798).

- **Respecting Feelings and Showing Kindness**
  Sensitivity to others' feelings helps create a harmonious community. Islam encourages Muslims to spread joy, compassion, and understanding.

- **Sincerity for Allah's Sake**
  Relationships and actions are ultimately for Allah's sake, not personal gain, ensuring that interactions remain genuine and purposeful.

11.2 Socializing and Building Community Bonds

Vaue of Social Interactions

Socializing, kindness, and participation in community activities are encouraged in Islam, as they cultivate patience, resilience, and empathy.

Guidelines for Social Interactions

- **Balance Social and Spiritual Life**
  While engaging with others, one should maintain focus on their faith and values.

- **Wish for Others What You Wish for Yourself**
  The Prophet (peace and blessings be upon him) said, "None of you truly believes until he loves for his brother what he loves for himself." (Sahih Bukhari, 13; Sahih Muslim 45). This selflessness fosters unity.

- **Sincere Compassion and Mercy**
  Compassion for others and a readiness to help reflects the Islamic spirit of solidarity.

- **Patiently Bear Harm and Forgive**
  Islam encourages forgiveness and patience, as Allah praises those who "restrain their anger and forgive others" (Qur'an 3:134).

- **Show Kindness Even When It's Not Reciprocated**
  Treating all with kindness, even those who may not return it, exemplifies Islam's moral strength.

11.3 Close Friendships

Loving for Allah's Sake

Loving others for Allah's sake completes one's faith and strengthens bonds of friendship.

Criteria for Close Friendship

- **Select Trustworthy Friends**
  Friends who uphold good values encourage a stronger faith and integrity.

- **Express Affection**
  The Prophet (peace and blessings be upon him) advised sharing feelings of affection with friends, creating warmth and trust.

- **Balance Love and Criticism**
  Excessive attachment or aversion can cloud judgment. Islam encourages moderate emotions as life circumstances may change.

- **Small Gestures of Kindness**
  Simple acts like giving gifts or expressing kind words reinforce friendship and strengthen the community.

11.4 Conduct in Gatherings

Proper etiquette in social gatherings maintains respect and fosters unity.

- **Arrive Prepared and Respect Others**
  Observing cleanliness and dressing well shows respect for those present.

- **Make Space and Show Humility**
  Allowing room for others and sitting humbly avoids making anyone feel left out or uncomfortable.

- **Respect the Gathering's Purpose**
  Refraining from private or exclusive conversations in a group promotes inclusivity.

- **Conclude with a Supplication**
  Ending with a prayer ensures that the gathering's benefits are maximized and that Allah's blessings accompany all.

11.5 Avoiding Estrangement

- **Prohibition Against Long-Lasting Grudges**
  Holding grudges for more than three days is discouraged, as it can damage community bonds. The Prophet (peace and blessings be upon him) said, "It is not permissible for a man to abandon his brother for more than three days." The one who seeks reconciliation first is rewarded for their humility and willingness to restore peace.

11.6 Hospitality

The Importance of Hospitality

Showing hospitality strengthens ties and fulfills a highly emphasized Sunnah.
- **Warmly Welcome Guests**
  Greeting guests warmly and showing respect fosters kindness and gratitude.

- **Serve Generously According to Means**
  Hospitality, even with limited resources, is an act of kindness and generosity.

- **Three Days of Hosting as Sunnah**
  Hosting for three days is encouraged, and further hospitality is seen as a charitable act.

11.7 Greetings (Assalamu Alaykum)

Etiquette of Giving Greetings

- **Initiate Greetings**
  Initiating greetings with "Assalamu Alaykum" and responding in kind builds familiarity and connection within the community. It is customary

for younger individuals to greet elders first and those who are walking to greet those who are sitting.

- **Return Greetings Respectfully**
  Islam teaches that returning a greeting is an obligation, helping ensure that all feel acknowledged and respected.

11.8 Responding to Sneezes

- **Proper Etiquette for Sneezing**
  When someone sneezes and praises Allah, responding with, "May Allah have mercy on you," and returning the prayer reinforces a spirit of care and respect within the community. The Prophet Muhammad (peace and blessings be upon him) said: "When one of you sneezes and praises Allah, then it is a duty upon every Muslim who hears him to say, 'May Allah have mercy on you (Yarhamuk Allah).'" The sneezer then replies, 'May Allah guide you and rectify your condition (Yahdikum Allah wa yuslihu balakum).'" (Sahih Bukhari, 6224; Sahih Muslim, 2991)

11.9 Invitations

Accepting Invitations

Attending invitations, especially for weddings, is a Sunnah. Declining invitations to gatherings with prohibited activities is, however, permitted.

- **Observe Etiquette as a Guest**
  Guests should sit where the host seats them, avoid intrusive questions, and seek permission before leaving.

11.10 Visiting the Sick

Etiquette of Visiting the Sick

- **Show Comfort and Kindness**
  Brief visits with sincere well-wishes comfort the sick and fulfill a praiseworthy Sunnah.

- **Pray for Health**: The Prophet Muhammad (peace and blessings be upon him) said: "No Muslim visits a sick Muslim in the morning except that seventy thousand angels send blessings upon him until evening, and if he visits him in the evening, seventy thousand angels send blessings upon him until morning, and he will have a garden in Paradise." (Sunan At-Tirmidhi, 969; Ibn Majah, 1442).

Conclusion

Islamic principles of kindness, sincerity, and respect foster a strong sense of community and brotherhood. Through thoughtful interactions, hospitality, and empathy, Muslims can fulfill the rights of others while cultivating a supportive, compassionate environment. These acts serve not only as social obligations but also as means to seek Allah's pleasure, creating a life of purpose and unity.

CHAPTER TWELVE

Rights of Specific Groups of People

In Islam, cultivating strong relationships with specific groups of people – such as relatives, parents, children, spouses, neighbors, and even members of the opposite sex – is essential for building a harmonious and supportive community. Loyalty (*wafa*) and modesty (*haya*) are core virtues that guide Muslims in respecting and honoring these bonds. This chapter delves into the rights and responsibilities Muslims have toward each group, fostering unity, kindness, and integrity.

12.1 Foundational Virtues – Loyalty and Modesty

- **Loyalty (Wafa')**
  Loyalty represents a deep commitment to honoring others' rights, particularly those closest to us. Family, neighbors, and close acquaintances deserve special care and respect.

- **Modesty (Haya')**
  Modesty, particularly in interactions with the opposite sex, preserves the purity of the heart and strengthens family bonds. This virtue extends to thoughts, actions, and appearance, setting boundaries that protect personal dignity and social respect.

12.2 Rights of Parents

- **Treating Parents with Excellence**
  Respect for parents is among the highest forms of worship in Islam.

Allah frequently mentions kindness to parents alongside His worship, underscoring their elevated status. Allah says: "And your Lord has decreed that you not worship except Him, and to parents, good treatment. Whether one or both of them reach old age [while] with you, say not to them [so much as], 'uff,' and do not repel them but speak to them a noble word. And lower to them the wing of humility out of mercy and say, 'My Lord, have mercy upon them as they brought me up [when I was] small.'" (Quran, Al-Isra 17:23-24).

- **Special Rights of the Mother**
  Mothers who endure physical and emotional sacrifices during pregnancy and childbirth hold a unique place in Islam. The Prophet (peace and blessings be upon him) emphasized that the mother's right is even greater than the father's due to her unique role in nurturing life. A man came to the Prophet Muhammad (peace and blessings be upon him) and asked: "O Messenger of Allah, who among the people is most deserving of my good company?" He said, "Your mother." The man asked, "Then who?" He said, "Your mother." The man asked again, "Then who?" He said, "Your mother." The man asked once more, "Then who?" He said, "Then your father." (Sahih al-Bukhari, 5971; Sahih Muslim, 2548)

- **Forms of Kindness Toward Parents**

1. **Praying for Them:** Regular prayers for parents reflect gratitude and honor for their sacrifices.

2. **Speaking Gently**: Speaking to parents with gentleness and kindness demonstrates respect and deepens familial bonds.

3. **Serving Them**: Assisting parents in their needs, whether in old age or daily life, is a means to earn their pleasure and Allah's favor.

12.3 Rights of Spouses

- **Mutual Rights and Responsibilities**
  Marriage in Islam is a partnership where both spouses are encouraged to treat each other with love, kindness, and respect. The Quran describes marriage as a relationship of "tranquility, love, and mercy" (Quran, Ar-Rum 30:21).

- **Family Planning**
  Spouses may mutually agree upon birth control or family planning methods, provided that no harm is involved and both parties consent.

- **Divorce Guidelines**
  Divorce, while permitted, is considered a last resort in Islam. Certain practices, like divorcing during menstruation, are discouraged, emphasizing that divorce should be approached with patience, reflection, and respect.

12.4 Rights of Children

- **Children as Blessings**
  Children are a source of joy, purpose, and reward in this life and the Hereafter. The Prophet (peace and blessings be upon him) encouraged marriage and procreation, emphasizing that raising righteous children contributes to a stronger community.

- **Key Practices for Newborns**
  Certain traditions, such as calling the *adhan* in the newborn's right ear, wrapping them in a clean cloth, and performing the *aqiqah* (sacrificial offering), introduce children into the Muslim faith and community.

The Prophet Muhammad (peace and blessings be upon him) said: "When a child is born to one of you, let him give the Adhan in his right ear and the Iqamah in his left ear, for it protects the child from Shaytan." (Sunan Abu Dawood, 5105).

The Prophet Muhammad (peace and blessings be upon him) said: "For the boy, two sheep, and for the girl, one sheep. It does not matter whether they are male or female." (Sunan Abu Dawood, 2834; Jami' at-Tirmidhi, 1513).

Another narration: "Every child is in pledge for its Aqiqah, which is sacrificed for it on the seventh day, and its head is shaved, and a name is given to it." (Sunan Abu Dawood, 2838).

- **Choosing Meaningful Names**
  Selecting good names with positive meanings reflects a family's hopes and intentions for the child's character and values.

- **Raising Children with Compassion**
  Islam encourages parents to raise children with kindness, patience, and mercy. Building their character with love and providing guidance

prepares them for independence and spiritual resilience.

12.5 Rights of Relatives

- **Importance of Maintaining Family Ties**
  Islam emphasizes the blessings of maintaining strong family relationships. The Prophet Muhammad (peace and blessings be upon him) said, "Whoever wishes for an increase in provision and a long life should maintain family ties." (Sahih Bukhari, 5985; Sahih Muslim, 2557)

- **Patience with Difficult Family Members**
  Family obligations remain, even when relatives may not be kind. Upholding patience and forgiveness in family interactions mirrors the teachings of the Prophet (peace and blessings be upon him), who encouraged treating others well despite difficulties. The Prophet Muhammad (peace and blessings be upon him) said: "The one who maintains ties is not the one who merely reciprocates. Rather, the one who truly maintains ties is the one who does so even when his relatives sever ties with him." (Sahih Bukhari, 5991)

- **Ways to Show Kindness to Family**
  Greeting family members, exchanging gifts, offering assistance, and holding respectful conversations are practical ways to express love and care within the family. The Prophet Muhammad (peace and blessings be upon him) said: "The best of you are those who are best to their families, and I am the best among you to my family." (Sunan At-Tirmidhi, 3895; Sunan Ibn Majah, 1977)

- **Avoiding Disrespect and Conflict**
  Avoiding behaviors that lead to disrespect or conflict among family members helps preserve unity. Keeping personal disagreements private, maintaining calm in discussions, and showing consideration in actions all foster stronger family bonds.

- **Regular Contact**
  Regular contact, through visits or calls, strengthens family bonds and shows a genuine interest in each other's well-being.

12.6 Rights of Neighbors

- **Value of Good Neighbors**
  The Prophet (peace and blessings be upon him) highlighted the importance of good neighbors, stating, "Choose your companion before the journey and your neighbor before the house." (Al-Adab Al-Mufrad, 113). Good neighbors enhance the quality of life and contribute to a supportive community.

- **Respecting Neighborly Rights**
  The rights of neighbors include showing them respect, offering assistance in times of need, and treating them well, regardless of their faith. Islam encourages Muslims to share food, offer support, and avoid actions that may disturb neighbors.

3. Practical Etiquette for Neighborly Relations
- **Offering Help and Support**
  Helping neighbors in need strengthens community ties and upholds compassion.

- **Avoiding Disturbances**
  Respecting neighbors' peace by avoiding loud noises or disruptive actions fosters harmony.

- **Maintaining a Friendly Demeanor**
  Simple gestures like smiling or greeting neighbors warmly can build trust and friendship.

- **Visiting in Times of Hardship**
  Offering condolences or assistance when neighbors face difficulties reflects Islamic values of empathy and kindness.

12.7 Interactions with the Opposite Sex

- **Observing Caution in Interactions**
  Interactions between men and women in Islam are framed by modesty and boundaries to prevent misunderstandings and maintain respect.

- **Lowering the Gaze**
  Lowering the gaze from prohibited sights helps maintain the purity of

the heart. The Prophet (peace be upon him) advised, "Do not follow a glance with another, for you will be forgiven for the first, but not for the second." (Sunan Abu Dawood, 2149; Jami' at-Tirmidhi, 2777).

- **Guidelines for Modesty with Non-Marriageable Kin**

Non-Marriageable Relations: Islam outlines specific rules for interactions with close relatives, ensuring respectful and modest behavior among family members.

Appropriate Dress: Modesty in dress is an essential part of respectful interaction. Young women are encouraged to cover themselves appropriately, while men are also urged to dress modestly to prevent inappropriate attention.

- **Restrictions on Physical Contact**
  Physical contact with non-marriageable kin of the opposite sex is generally limited, except in cases of necessity, and touching is discouraged without valid reasons.

- **Rules on Being Alone (Khalwa)**
  A man and a woman who are not closely related should avoid being alone together unless a barrier or third party is present to prevent potential misconduct and protect the dignity of both parties.

Conclusion

In Islam, respecting the rights of specific groups is a pathway to a balanced and compassionate life. Through loyalty and modesty, Muslims honor the bonds of family, marriage, neighborhood, and respectful interactions between genders. These teachings offer guidance on treating others with love, respect, and care, contributing to a thriving, supportive community where each person's rights are preserved.

CHAPTER THIRTEEN

Guidelines for Speech

In Islam, speech is viewed as a powerful tool that shapes relationships, conveys values, and can either uplift or harm. Responsible, respectful communication is a core principle that helps maintain harmony within the community and strengthens one's connection to Allah. This chapter outlines guidelines for ethical and purposeful speech, encouraging Muslims to be mindful of the impact of their words.

13.1 General Principles for Speech

Silence as a Virtue

Silence is highly valued in Islam, as it helps prevent conflict, sins, and unnecessary disputes. The Prophet Muhammad (peace and blessings be upon him) said, "Whoever remains silent is safe." (Sunan At-Tirmidhi, 2501). Practicing silence fosters reflection, self-control, and peace of mind.

Speaking Meaningfully

When speaking, one should focus on remembering Allah, promoting good, and preventing harm. Idle or frivolous talk distracts from one's purpose and can waste time and energy. The Prophet (peace and blessings be upon him) taught, "Whoever believes in Allah and the Last Day, let him speak good or remain silent. And whoever believes in Allah and the Last Day, let him honor his neighbor. And whoever believes in Allah and the Last Day, let him honor his guest." (Sahih Bukhari, 6018; Sahih Muslim, 47).

Using a Gentle Tone

Speaking in a gentle, moderate tone reflects humility and respect. The Qur'an advises, "Lower your voice; the harshest of voices is the braying of donkeys." (Quran, Luqman 31:19).

Clear and Concise Speech

The Prophet (peace and blessings be upon him) modeled clear and concise speech, expressing himself in a way that was easily understood by listeners.

Adding "Insha'Allah" (God Willing)

Including "Insha'Allah" when discussing future actions acknowledges Allah's will and keeps one grounded in humility and faith.

Truthfulness

Honesty is a pillar of Islamic ethics. A believer should speak the truth even if it brings hardship, as complete faith requires integrity. As the Prophet (peace and blessings be upon him) advised, "Truthfulness leads to righteousness, and righteousness leads to Paradise. A man continues to tell the truth until he is recorded with Allah as a truthful person. Lying leads to wickedness, and wickedness leads to the Hellfire. A man continues to lie until he is recorded with Allah as a liar." (Sahih Bukhari, 6094; Sahih Muslim, 2607).

13.2 Avoiding Lying

The Gravity of Lying

Lying is prohibited in Islam, as it can harm others and lead to greater sins. The Prophet (peace and blessings be upon him) said, "Lying leads to wickedness, and wickedness leads to Hell." (Sahih Bukhari, 6094; Sahih Muslim, 2607). This applies whether lying is done seriously or as a joke.

Forms of Serious Lies

- **Lying about Allah or His Messenger** (peace and blessings be upon him): Considered the gravest lie.

- **Bearing False Witness**: Giving false testimony, especially in legal matters, is a major sin.

- **False Accusations**: Accusing a chaste person of immorality is particularly condemned.

Permissible Lies

In Islam, lying is permitted only in rare cases:
- In warfare for tactical reasons.

- To reconcile feuding parties.

- To bring peace within a marriage or to please one's spouse in a non-deceptive way.

13.3 Avoiding Backbiting (Ghiba)

Definition of Backbiting

Backbiting means mentioning someone's faults behind their back in a way they would dislike, even if it is true. This is a major sin that damages trust and community ties.

Permissible Cases for Backbiting

Exceptions include seeking justice, warning others of harm, or giving advice to protect others. However, the intent must be pure and focused on preventing harm rather than belittling someone.

Making Amends

If backbiting has harmed someone, the person should seek their forgiveness. Otherwise, sincere repentance and remorse are necessary for atonement.

13.4 Avoiding Tale-Bearing (Namima)

Definition of Tale-Bearing

Tale-bearing is spreading information with the intent to create discord. This behavior is strictly prohibited in Islam, as it leads to conflict and mistrust.

Privacy and Confidentiality

Preserving others' privacy is a duty, and information should only be shared if it serves a legitimate purpose, such as preventing harm.

13.5 Joking with Caution

Guidelines for Joking

Joking is permissible when it is truthful, gentle, and does not mock or scare others. Excessive joking, however, diminishes respect and can strain relationships.

13.6 Avoiding Mocking (Sukhriyya)

Mocking, imitating, or belittling others is prohibited, as it can harm others' dignity. The Quran warns, "Let not one group mock another; perhaps they may be better than them" (Quran, Al-Hujurat 49:11). Muslims are encouraged to foster a respectful and compassionate environment, free from ridicule.

13.7 Avoiding Cursing (La'n)

Restrictions on Cursing

Cursing specific individuals is forbidden unless they are confirmed to have died outside Islam. Cursing inanimate objects or animals is also discouraged.

Cursing Actions, Not People

It is permissible to curse sinful behaviors in general, as this discourages evil acts without attacking specific individuals.

13.8 Avoiding Insulting (Sabb)

Insulting others is forbidden in Islam. One may reply within respectful limits if insulted, but forgiveness is preferred. The Prophet (peace be upon him) encouraged kindness, even in response to hostility.

13.9 Faultfinding

Finding faults or criticizing others unnecessarily is discouraged. The Quran advises, "Do not defame one another." (Quran, Al-Hujurat 49:11). Encouraging others' strengths rather than highlighting their weaknesses fosters unity and respect within the community.

13.10 Avoiding Vulgarity

Vulgar or obscene language, especially concerning sensitive matters, is disrespectful and should be avoided. The Prophet (peace and blessings be upon him) said, "The believer is not a slanderer, nor does he curse others, nor is he immoral or foul." (Jami` at-Tirmidhi, 1977; Musnad Ahmad, 3839).
Clean and respectful language reflects inner purity and respect for others.

13.11 Refraining from Nitpicking (Mira')

Picking apart others' words or nitpicking without reason is discouraged. The Prophet (peace and blessings be upon him) said, "I guarantee a house in Paradise for the one who gives up arguing, even if he is right; and a house in the middle of Paradise for the one who abandons lying, even in jest; and a house in the highest part of Paradise for the one who makes his character excellent." (Sunan Abu Dawood, 4800). Muslims are encouraged to be understanding and avoid excessive scrutiny.

13.12 Constructive Argumentation (Jidal)

Argumentation meant to display one's intelligence or to humiliate is prohibited. However, arguing gently to clarify or spread truth is permitted if it aims to build understanding, not to provoke conflict. Allah says, "And argue with them with that which is best" (Quran, Al-Nahl 16:125).

13.13 Speaking of Immorality

Discussing sinful or immoral activities is discouraged, as it may promote harm or affect others' morals negatively. A Muslim's words should uplift, educate, or guide, avoiding topics that could lead to spiritual or ethical harm.

13.14 Praise with Care

Limit Excessive Praise

Excessive praise can lead to arrogance and is discouraged. When praising, it's preferable to use humble phrases like, "I believe him to be..." to avoid instilling pride in others.

Purposeful Praise

Praise is commendable when done to encourage good deeds or inspire others positively, without fostering arrogance.

13.15 Swearing Oaths

Avoid Frequent Swearing by Allah

Frequent swearing by Allah's name can diminish reverence for it. Breaking an oath requires expiation to honor Allah's name and respect for promises.

Limiting Swearing to Allah Alone

Swearing by Allah alone and avoiding oaths by other entities maintains respect for the Creator.

13.16 Commanding Good and Forbidding Evil

Obligation and Responsibility

Commanding good and preventing harm is a communal duty if one has the knowledge, patience, and compassion necessary to advise others correctly.

Qualities of Effective Counselors

The person enjoining good should be gentle, patient, and knowledgeable, ensuring their advice aligns with Islamic principles and is given sincerely.

Conclusion

Islamic guidelines for speech encourage responsibility, honesty, and humility. Muslims are called to use their words to promote good, avoid harm, and reflect Islamic values of kindness, respect, and modesty. By upholding these guidelines, believers honor their faith and build a harmonious community while strengthening their personal connection to Allah.

CHAPTER FOURTEEN

Guidelines for Conduct in Specific Places

I n Islam, places carry significance, and respectful behavior within them enhances both individual and community well-being. Whether on the road or in a mosque, mindful conduct reflects Islamic values of compassion, respect, and humility. This chapter provides guidelines for upholding decorum in these places, as drawn from the Prophetic example.

14.1 Walking and Rights of the Road

Prayer for Safety and Guidance When Leaving Home

As one leaves home, they should say, "In the name of Allah; I place my trust in Allah; there is no power or strength except with Allah." The Prophet Muhammad (peace and blessings be upon him) taught that this prayer grants protection, guidance, and safety, serving as a reminder of one's reliance on Allah in all daily encounters. The Prophet (peace and blessings be upon him) said: "Whoever says, when he leaves his house: 'In the name of Allah; I place my trust in Allah; there is no power or strength except with Allah' (la hawla wala quwwata illa billah,' it will be said to him: 'You are guided, defended, and protected.' The devils will go far away from him." (Sunan Abu Dawood, 5095; Jami` at-Tirmidhi, 3426).

Seeking Protection from Harm

Seeking refuge in Allah from misguidance, oppression, and ignorance is a recommended practice. The Prophet (peace and blessings be upon him) would recite a supplication for safety whenever leaving a place, illustrating a proactive approach to seeking Allah's protection.

Walking with Humility and Courtesy

One should walk with a sense of humility, avoiding excessive gestures, and leaving space for others on pathways, particularly for women and the elderly. This humble gait reflects self-restraint and respect for the people one encounters.

Clearing Obstacles from the Path

Removing hazards such as sharp objects, stones, or other obstacles from the road is considered an act of charity. The Prophet (peace and blessings be upon him) praised those who clear the path for others, highlighting this simple yet impactful act as an act of kindness rewarded by Allah. "Removing harmful things from the road is an act of charity." (Sahih Bukhari, 2989; Sahih Muslim, 1009).

Limiting Time in Marketplaces

Islam recommends minimizing time in marketplaces where distractions are common. Visiting the marketplace should be purposeful, avoiding idle time to prevent indulgence in unnecessary or distracting activities. The Prophet Muhammad (peace and blessings be upon him) said: "The most beloved of places to Allah are the mosques, and the most hated places to Allah are the markets." (Sahih Muslim, 671; Sunan an-Nasa'i, 693).

Observing the Rights of the Road

If one is sitting or walking along a road, it is essential to observe the following guidelines:

- **Lowering the Gaze**: Avoid looking at others inappropriately.

- **Avoiding Harm**: Prevent harm or disturbance to others.

- **Responding to Greetings**: Reply to those who greet you with warmth.

- **Promoting Good and Preventing Harm**: Encourage positive behavior and speak out against wrongdoings.

- **Assisting Those in Need**: Offer support to those who require help.

- **Guiding the Lost**: Provide directions to those seeking guidance.

- **Respecting Cleanliness**: Maintain cleanliness by refraining from littering or spitting.

Showing Humility While Riding or Walking in Public

Avoid creating an impression of superiority by walking or riding in a way that implies entitlement. The Prophet (peace and blessings be upon him) valued humility in public spaces and warned against ostentatious behavior.

Helping Those with Disabilities

Offer a helping hand to those with disabilities, such as guiding a blind person safely across the road. Acts of assistance strengthen bonds within the community and reflect empathy and kindness.

Extending Greetings to Fellow Muslims

One should greet fellow Muslims warmly, regardless of familiarity, as greeting enhances unity and love within the community. The Prophet (peace be upon him) said that exchanging greetings (salam) increases affection among Muslims.

14.2 Conduct in Mosques

Walking to the Mosque with Reverence

When heading to the mosque, one should walk calmly and with humility, hoping for Allah's reward with every step. Entering the mosque in a state of inner and outer purity, with cleansed footwear and respectful attire, reflects respect for the sacredness of the place.

Entering and Exiting the Mosque

Enter with humility, praising Allah and sending blessings upon the Prophet (peace and blessings be upon him). It is recommended to avoid leaving the mosque without first offering prayer or engaging in remembrance as a way of honoring the sanctity of the space.

Maintaining Proper Conduct Inside

The mosque is a place of worship, and worldly discussions should be minimized. Arguing or raising one's voice is discouraged. Additionally, activities like paid work, trading, and buying or selling should not occur in the mosque, as they distract from the mosque's primary purpose.

Cleanliness and Respect for the Mosque's Space

Maintaining the mosque's cleanliness is vital. Refrain from spitting on the floor or bringing in impure substances. The Prophet (peace and blessings be upon him) emphasized that mosques should be kept free from dirt and foul odors, preserving their sanctity.

Conduct with Children and Pets

Young children may enter the mosque if they can maintain cleanliness and quiet. However, if there is a risk of disruption, it is preferable to leave them outside to avoid disturbing others.

Appropriate Seating and Movement

Respect others' personal space by avoiding unnecessary crowding, stepping over people's necks, or blocking pathways during gatherings. Keeping pathways clear ensures comfort for all worshippers.

Respect for Those Praying

Avoid walking in front of someone engaged in prayer, as it disrupts their connection with Allah. This act respects the concentration and serenity of others during their worship. The Prophet (peace and blessings be upon him) said: "If anyone of you arrives at the mosque and the people are praying, let him not step over their necks but sit wherever he finds space." (Sunan Abu Dawud, 1114).

Approach to Beggars in the Mosque

Offering support to beggars who disturb worshippers by stepping over them is discouraged, as it detracts from the prayerful atmosphere.

Respecting the Mosque's Sacredness

Certain actions, such as marital intimacy or relieving oneself, should never occur on mosque premises out of respect for the mosque's sanctity. The Prophet (peace be upon him) stressed that the mosque is solely for worship. The Prophet Muhammad (peace and blessings be upon him) said: "When one of you enters the mosque, let him not sit until he has prayed two units of prayer." (Sahih Bukhari, 1167; Sahih Muslim, 714). Additionally, the Prophet (peace and blessings be upon him) said: "The mosques are built for the remembrance of Allah, prayer, and recitation of the Quran." (Sahih Muslim, 285).

Avoiding Foul Odors in the Mosque

To maintain a clean and pleasant atmosphere, avoid entering the mosque with foul-smelling substances like garlic or onion. Respecting this guideline shows consideration for the comfort of others. The Prophet Muhammad (peace and blessings be upon him) said: "Whoever eats garlic or onion, let him keep away from us, or keep away from our mosque, and stay in his house." (Sahih al-Bukhari, 855; Sahih Muslim, 564). In another narration: "The angels are offended by that which offends the sons of Adam." (Sahih Muslim, 564).

Proper Use of Mosque Facilities

Ablution should be performed in designated areas, as the water used is considered impure. This practice keeps the prayer space clean and free from distractions.

Conclusion

Whether on the road or in a mosque, Islam emphasizes respectful and considerate behavior toward others and toward the space itself. Humility, compassion, and assistance to others are encouraged in public places. In the mosque, a worshipper's conduct should reflect reverence, modesty, and cleanliness. By following these guidelines, Muslims can embody the values of their faith in all aspects of daily life, fostering community harmony and drawing closer to Allah.

CHAPTER FIFTEEN

Honoring the Rights of the Universe

I slamic teachings emphasize the importance of honoring all elements of creation. The concept of "rights of the universe" reflects a holistic approach to worship and stewardship, reminding us that our responsibility as Muslims extends beyond human interactions to include the environment, animals, and all of Allah's creations. Living Islam with purpose involves respecting and caring for the world around us, preserving it for future generations, and appreciating it as a manifestation of Allah's wisdom and power.

15.1 Respecting the Earth

Appreciation of Earth as a Sacred Trust

The Earth is a sacred trust bestowed upon us by Allah, intended for responsible use and care. The Quran states: "And do not cause corruption upon the earth after its reformation." (Quran, Al-A'raf 7:56)

This verse calls on Muslims to avoid harmful practices that disrupt the natural balance, reflecting the Qur'anic principle of stewardship (*khalifah*). Responsible actions, such as reducing waste, recycling, and sustainable living, align with the teachings of Islam by protecting Earth's resources and acknowledging their role as divine blessings.

Conserving Resources

Islam emphasizes conservation and mindful consumption. Even in acts of worship, the Prophet Muhammad (peace be upon him) advocated moderation, saying, "Do not waste water, even if performing ablution on the banks of a flowing river." (Musnad Ahmad, 6768; Sunan Ibn Majah, 425). This teaches us to value resources like water and avoid waste, embodying gratitude for the provisions Allah has bestowed upon us.

Planting and Cultivating with Intention

The Prophet (peace be upon him) encouraged planting trees and nurturing the earth as an ongoing charity (*sadaqah jariyah*). He said, "If a Muslim plants a tree or sows seeds, and then a bird, or a person, or an animal eats from it, it is regarded as a charitable gift (Sadaqah)." (Sahih Bukhari, 2320; Sahih Muslim, 1552). This highlights the spiritual reward in nurturing life and the ethical significance of planting trees, fostering a sense of responsibility toward the environment and its inhabitants.

15.2 Rights of Animals

Compassionate Treatment of Animals

Animals are part of Allah's creation and have rights that must be respected. The Prophet (peace and blessings be upon him) said, "Whoever is merciful even to a sparrow, Allah will be merciful to him on the Day of Judgment." (Musnad Ahmad, 7001; Shu'ab al-Iman, 7461). "Verily, Allah has prescribed excellence in everything. If you slaughter, then slaughter well; and if you kill, then kill well. Let each one of you sharpen his blade and spare suffering to the animal he slaughters." (Sahih Muslim, 1955). "Do not make any living being the target of your arrows." (Sahih Muslim, 1958; Sahih Bukhari, 5515). This underscores the importance of treating all creatures with kindness and mercy, reflecting a fundamental aspect of Islamic ethics.

Proper Care for Domesticated Animals

Islam mandates that animals under human care, such as pets or livestock, must have proper food, shelter, and rest. The Prophet (peace be upon him) condemned the mistreatment of animals, illustrating that the care of animals is a reflection of one's faith and compassion. The Prophet Muhammad (peace and blessings be upon him) said: "A woman was punished in Hell because of a cat which she had confined until it died. She did not give it to eat or drink when it was confined, nor did she free it so that it might eat the insects of the earth." (Sahih Bukhari, 2365; Sahih Muslim, 2242).

Ethical Use of Animals

Islam permits using animals for lawful purposes, such as food, but strictly emphasizes ethical treatment. The Prophet (peace and blessings be upon him) taught that animals should not be overburdened, abused, or slaughtered in a way that causes unnecessary suffering, ensuring that human needs are balanced with compassion and respect for animals. The Prophet (peace and blessings be upon him) said: "Fear Allah in regard to these mute animals. Ride them while they are in good condition, and eat them while they are in good condition." (Sunan Abu Dawood, 2548).

15.3 Atmosphere and Air

Maintaining the Cleanliness of the Air

Islam calls on Muslims to avoid actions that contribute to air pollution and environmental harm. The Quran warns against activities that cause corruption and destruction, such as excessive fuel burning and improper waste disposal, reminding us that our actions impact the well-being of all creation. "And do not cause corruption upon the earth after its reformation."(Quran, Al-A'raf, 7:56). "And do not commit abuse on the earth, spreading corruption." (Quran, Al-Baqarah, 2:60). "And it is He who has made you successors upon the earth." (Quran, Al-An'am, 6:165).

Preserving Natural Beauty for Worship and Well-Being

Islam encourages preserving the natural environment, which fosters physical health and spiritual clarity. Clean air and a pure environment enhance concentration, reflection, and overall health, aligning with the Islamic emphasis on physical and spiritual well-being.

15.4 Water Conservation

Water as a Precious Resource

Water is the source of all life, as noted in the Quran: "We made from water every living thing." (Qur'an, Al-Anbiya' 21:30)

   Islamic teachings underscore water's sacredness, urging Muslims to avoid waste and protect water sources. By conserving and sharing water, we express gratitude for this essential blessing.

Ensuring Water Access for All Creatures

The Prophet (peace and blessings be upon him) praised those who provide water to others, including animals, as an act of kindness and charity. Offering water to any living being is highly rewarded, emphasizing the right of all creatures to this vital resource.

15.5 Wilderness and Wildlife

Protecting Wildlife and Natural Habitats

Natural areas, forests, and ecosystems are valuable in their own right as part of Allah's creation. Islam encourages the preservation of biodiversity and discourages actions that destroy habitats or harm wildlife.

Avoiding Unnecessary Harm to Wildlife

Unnecessary harm to animals, whether through hunting, deforestation, or other destructive actions, is discouraged in Islam. The Prophet (peace and blessings be upon him) said, "Whoever kills a sparrow or anything smaller without a just cause, Allah will question him about it on the Day of Judgment" (Sunan an-Nasa'i, 4446; Musnad Ahmad, 19444), stressing the significance of intentional and compassionate actions.

Recognizing Nature as a Reflection of Allah

The Quran invites believers to contemplate the natural world as a testament to Allah's beauty and wisdom. Observing the intricacies of nature deepens one's appreciation for Allah's creativity, fostering a love for the Creator and a commitment to preserving His creation.

15.6 The Night Sky and Celestial Bodies

Contemplating the Stars and Heavens

The Quran encourages contemplation of the stars, sun, and moon as reminders of Allah's greatness. Reflecting on the heavens cultivates a sense of wonder and humility, reinforcing our connection to the Creator.

Signs in the Heavens: "Indeed, in the creation of the heavens and the earth, and the alternation of the night and the day, are signs for those of understanding." (Quran, Aal-E-Imran, 3:190).

The Sun and Moon as Signs: "And He subjected for you the sun and the moon, continuous [in orbit], and subjected for you the night and the day." (Quran, Ibrahim, 14:33).

Stars for Guidance and Beauty: "And it is He who placed for you the stars that you may be guided by them the darknesses of the land and sea. We have detailed the signs for a people who know." (Quran, Al-An'am, 6:97). "Indeed, We have adorned the nearest heaven with an adornment of stars." (Quran, As-Saffat, 37:6).

The Sun and Moon in Perfect Measure: "The sun and the moon [move] by precise calculation, and the stars and trees prostrate." (Quran, Ar-Rahman, 55:5-6).

Celestial Movements as Evidence of Allah: "And the sun runs [on course] toward its stopping point. That is the determination of the Exalted in Might, the Knowing. And the moon - We have determined its phases until it returns [appearing] like the old date stalk." (Quran Ya-Sin, 36:38-39).

Recognizing Celestial Phenomena in Worship

In Islam, observing the moon's phases is essential for determining the timing of Ramadan and other sacred periods, linking the natural world to our worship practices. This awareness of celestial cycles aligns our lives with the natural order Allah has established, promoting harmony with creation.

Conclusion: Living Islam by Fulfilling the Rights of the Universe

Honoring the universe as Allah's creation enriches our faith and reinforces our role as caretakers of the Earth. By respecting the rights of the Earth, animals, air, water, wilderness, and celestial bodies, we draw closer to Allah, fostering harmony and well-being for ourselves and the world around us. Living Islam purposefully means upholding these rights with intention, as every respectful act we perform—whether conserving water, planting a tree, showing compassion to animals, or marveling at the stars—reflects our commitment to the Creator and enhances the beauty and balance of His creation.

CHAPTER SIXTEEN

Regular Devotions and Reciting the Quran

Regular devotions and the recitation of the Quran are central to a believer's spiritual life, serving as a means of connecting with Allah and maintaining a state of mindfulness and purity. Imam al-Haddad, in his *Book of Assistance*, emphasizes the recitation of specific surahs at particular times, as these surahs hold profound spiritual significance and benefits. This chapter explores the importance of regular devotions, practical tips for Quranic recitation, and the surahs recommended by Imam al-Haddad.

16.1 Regular Devotions and Daily Structure

Morning and Evening Dhikr

Imam al-Haddad stresses the importance of beginning and ending each day with the remembrance of Allah, which includes the recitation of specific surahs. These practices protect the soul, bring blessings to one's time, and help a believer maintain their focus on Allah.

- **Surah Ya-Sin (Chapter 36):** Recommended for recitation in the early morning to start the day with spiritual blessings and ease in one's endeavors. The Prophet Muhammad (peace and blessings be upon him) referred to it as the "heart of the Quran." "Surely, everything has a heart, and the heart of the Quran is Ya-Sin. I would love for it to be in the heart of every believer." (Sunan At-Tirmidhi, 2887).

- **Surah Al-Waqi'ah (Chapter 56):** Recited in the evening to safeguard against poverty and to remind oneself of the realities of the Hereafter. "Whoever recites Surah Al-Waqiah every night will never be afflicted by poverty." (Sunan Ibn Majah, 9250)

Before Sleep

The nighttime routine is crucial to fortifying one's relationship with Allah. Imam al-Haddad suggests the following surahs and verses:

- **Surah Al-Mulk (Chapter 67):** Recited before sleep to earn Allah's protection from the punishment of the grave. The Prophet (peace and blessings be upon him) said: "There is a surah in the Quran, consisting of thirty verses, that will intercede for its companion until he is forgiven: 'Blessed is He in Whose Hand is the dominion' (Surah Al-Mulk)." (Sunan Abu Dawood, Hadith 1400; Jami` at-Tirmidhi, 2891). In another narration: "It (Surah Al-Mulk) is a protector; it saves from the punishment of the grave." (Sunan Ibn Majah, 3786).

- **Surah As-Sajdah (Chapter 32):** Often paired with Surah Al-Mulk for its reminder of the greatness of Allah and the importance of submission to Him.

- **The Last Two Ayahs of Surah Al-Baqarah (2:285–286):** These ayahs protect throughout the night, encompassing trust in Allah and reliance on Him. The Prophet Muhammad (peace and blessings be upon him) said: "Whoever recites the last two verses of Surah Al-Baqarah at night, it will suffice him." (Sahih Bukhari, 5009; Sahih Muslim, 807).

After Prayer

For increased blessings and spiritual fortification, Imam al-Haddad recommends:

- **Ayat Al-Kursi (2:255):** Recited after every obligatory prayer to seek protection and blessings. This ayah is a powerful affirmation of Allah's sovereignty and care. The Prophet Muhammad (peace and blessings be upon him) said: "Whoever recites Ayat Al-Kursi after every obligatory prayer, nothing stands between him and Paradise except death." (Sunan An-Nasa'i, 9847; Ibn Hibban, 1002). Another narration: "When you go to your bed, recite Ayat Al-Kursi, for there will be a guardian appointed over you from Allah, and no devil will approach you until morning." (Sahih Bukhari, 2311).

- **Surah Al-Ikhlas (Chapter 112), Al-Falaq (Chapter 113), and An-Nas (Chapter 114):** Recited three times each after Fajr and Maghrib prayers for protection from harm and spiritual fortification. The Prophet Muhammad (peace and blessings be upon him) said: "Say: 'Surah Al-Ikhlas,' and the two Surahs of protection (Al-Falaq and An-Naas) three times in the morning and evening; they will suffice you for everything." (Sunan Abu Dawood, 5082; Jami` at-Tirmidhi, 3575).

16.2 Special Times and Their Recommended Surahs

Friday (Jumu'ah)

The day of Friday holds special significance in Islam, and Imam al-Haddad encourages devoting extra time to Quranic recitation and reflection. On this blessed day:

- **Surah Al-Kahf (Chapter 18):** Recited either on the night before (Thursday evening) or during the day of Friday for illumination and protection from the trials of the Dajjal. The Prophet Muhammad (peace and blessings be upon him) said: "Whoever recites Surah Al-Kahf on the day of Jumu'ah (Friday), will have a light that will shine from him from one Friday to the next." (Sunan Al-Kubra Al-Bayhaqi, 5856). He (peace and blessings be upon him) also said: "Whoever memorizes ten ayah from the beginning of Surah Al-Kahf will be protected from the trial of the Dajjal." (Sahih Muslim, 809).

- **Surah As-Saffat (Chapter 37):** Recommended for recitation on Friday morning to start the day with blessings and as a reminder of the stories of the Prophets.

Other Times

- **Surah Ad-Dukhan (Chapter 44):** Recommended for recitation on Thursday night to seek forgiveness and blessings from Allah. The Prophet (peace and blessings be upon him) is reported to have said: "Whoever recites Surah Ad-Dukhan on the night of Friday, Allah will forgive him." (Sunan At-Tirmidhi, 2889; Sunan Ad-Darimi, 3406).

- **Surah Al-Hashr (Chapter 59), especially Verses 22–24:** Recite these verses regularly to deepen your understanding of Allah's names and attributes.

16.3 Practical Guidelines for Reciting Recommended Surahs

- **Consistency Over Quantity:** Imam al-Haddad emphasizes that it is better to recite a small portion of the Quran regularly and with sincerity than to recite large portions inconsistently or without focus.

- **Proper Intention:** Approach the Quran with the intention of seeking Allah's pleasure, guidance, and mercy.

- **Reflection and Understanding:** Take time to ponder the meanings of the verses you recite, as this deepens the spiritual impact of the Quran on your heart and actions.

- **Physical and Spiritual Cleanliness:** Perform wudu' before reciting the Quran, sit in a clean place, and recite with humility and reverence.

16.4 The Comprehensive Devotional Program

To benefit from the Quran fully, Imam al-Haddad advises integrating these surahs into your daily and weekly routine. Below is a suggested structure based on his recommendations:

1. **Daily:**

   - Morning: Surah Ya-Sin

   - Evening: Surah Al-Waqi'ah

   - After every obligatory prayer: Ayat Al-Kursi

   - Night before sleeping: Surah Al-Mulk, Surah As-Sajdah, and the last two verses of Surah Al-Baqarah

2. **Weekly:**

   - Thursday Night: Surah Ad-Dukhan

   - Friday Morning: Surah As-Saffat

   - Friday Day: Surah Al-Kahf

3. **Regularly:**

   - Surah Al-Ikhlas, Al-Falaq, and An-Nas (daily after Fajr and Maghrib)

   - Verses 22–24 of Surah Al-Hashr for reflecting on Allah's names and attributes.

Conclusion

The Quran is a treasure trove of guidance, mercy, and blessings, and its regular recitation, as outlined by Imam al-Haddad, enriches the believer's life both spiritually and practically. By incorporating these recommended surahs into your daily and weekly routine, you strengthen your relationship with Allah, protect yourself from harm, and align your heart with the teachings of Islam. Let the words of Allah illuminate your path and inspire your journey to the Hereafter.

CHAPTER SEVENTEEN

A Day in the Life of a Muslim: Integrating Faith into Modern Routines

I n today's fast-paced world, filled with endless responsibilities and distractions, Muslims often strive to maintain a balance between their worldly duties and their spiritual obligations. Islam provides a comprehensive guide to integrating worship, mindfulness, and ethical conduct into daily routines, enabling believers to remain connected to Allah while fulfilling their responsibilities. This chapter explores a typical day in the life of a Muslim, offering practical insights on aligning daily routines with Islamic values, incorporating time for learning Islam and reciting the Quran, and nurturing a meaningful connection with Allah.

17.1 Morning: Starting the Day with Purpose and Gratitude

The Morning's Spiritual Importance

Morning in Islam is a time of renewal, gratitude, and spiritual reflection. The Prophet Muhammad (peace and blessings be upon him) said, "The two rak'ahs (units) before Fajr are better than the world and all that is in it" (Sahih Muslim, 725; Sunan At-Tirmidhi, 418).

. This statement highlights the unique blessings associated with the early hours of the day.

Fajr Prayer: A Fresh Start

The day begins before sunrise with Fajr, the dawn prayer. Rising early for Fajr instills discipline and reminds Muslims of their commitment to Allah. This sacred time is often accompanied by *dhikr* (remembrance of Allah) and *du'a* (supplication), allowing believers to seek Allah's blessings and guidance for the day ahead.

Morning Adhkar and Reflection

After Fajr, Muslims often recite the **morning** *adhkar*, a set of supplications for protection, gratitude, and mindfulness. For example, the supplication: *"O Allah, by Your permission, we have reached the morning, and by Your permission, we will reach the evening"* sets the tone for a day centered around reliance on Allah. These moments are ideal for reflecting on personal goals and aligning daily tasks with Islamic principles.

Quran Recitation and Study

Early morning is an optimal time for engaging with the Quran. Many Muslims dedicate this time to reciting a *Juz* (one part) of the Quran daily. Completing a *Juz* each day allows Muslims to finish the Quran in a month while contemplating its meanings. Reflecting on verses or studying tafsir (Quranic exegesis) enhances understanding and strengthens the bond with Allah's words.

Physical and Mental Well-being

Islam emphasizes the importance of physical health as a trust from Allah. Incorporating light exercise or a morning walk invigorates the body and mind. A healthy breakfast, coupled with gratitude for Allah's provisions, transforms a mundane activity into an act of worship.

17.2 Mid-Morning: Balancing Work, Study, and Worship

Setting Intentions

Before beginning work, study, or household tasks, Muslims are encouraged to set clear intentions. The Prophet Muhammad (peace and blessings be upon him) said, "Actions are judged by intentions, and every person will get the reward according to what he has intended. So whoever emigrated for Allah and His Messenger, his emigration will be for Allah and His Messenger. And whoever emigrated for worldly reasons or to marry a woman, his emigration will be for what he emigrated for." (Sahih Bukhari, 1; Sahih Muslim, 1907). This simple act of intention transforms daily responsibilities into acts of worship, ensuring that even mundane tasks contribute to spiritual growth.

Dedicating Time to Islamic Learning

Mid-morning is an excellent period to focus on learning about Islam. Whether studying the Quran, reading Hadith, or attending a class on Islamic jurisprudence, this time allows for spiritual enrichment. Memorizing Quranic verses or exploring the life of the Prophet (peace and blessings be upon him) inspires greater devotion and understanding of Islamic principles.

Dhikr and Mindfulness Breaks

Amid work or study, short breaks for *dhikr* refresh the mind and strengthen spiritual awareness. Reciting phrases like *"SubhanAllah"* (Glory be to Allah), *"Alhamdulillah"* (All praise is due to Allah), and *"Allahu Akbar"* (Allah is greater) brings peace and reminds Muslims of their ultimate purpose.

Upholding Ethics in Responsibilities

Islam emphasizes the importance of honesty, diligence, and fairness in all dealings. Muslims embody Islamic values by treating colleagues and clients with respect, avoiding gossip, and demonstrating integrity. This approach not only pleases Allah but also leaves a positive impact on those around them.

17.3 Afternoon: Rejuvenation and Realignment

Dhuhr Prayer: A Midday Anchor

Dhuhr, the midday prayer, offers a spiritual pause to reconnect with Allah and realign intentions. This act of worship reminds Muslims to maintain a balance between their worldly tasks and their spiritual goals.

Gratitude During Lunch

Lunch provides an opportunity to express gratitude. Saying *"Bismillah"* before eating and *"Alhamdulillah"* afterward transforms a simple meal into an act of worship. Sharing food with family, friends, or colleagues fosters community bonds and reflects the Islamic value of generosity.

Balancing Responsibilities

The afternoon is often filled with tasks, from professional duties to managing household responsibilities. By renewing intentions and seeking Allah's help, Muslims can approach their roles with sincerity and patience. For instance, fulfilling a job responsibility with diligence and kindness becomes a means of earning Allah's reward.

17.4 Evening: Family, Worship, and Growth

Asr Prayer: Spiritual and Emotional Reflection

Asr, the late afternoon prayer, serves as a reminder of the day's nearing end. The Prophet Muhammad (peace and blessings be upon him) said, "Whoever prays the two cool prayers (Fajr and Asr) will enter Paradise" (Sahih Bukhari, 574; Sahih Muslim, 635). This prayer encourages believers to reflect on their progress, seek forgiveness for shortcomings, and recommit to their intentions.

Family Time: Strengthening Bonds

Evenings are often spent with family, a cornerstone of Islamic life. Whether sharing a meal, helping children with homework, or discussing the day's events, these moments strengthen family ties and embody the Prophet's teaching: "The best of you are those who are best to their families, and I am the best among you to my family." (Sunan At-Tirmidhi, 3895; Sunan Ibn Majah, 1977).

Personal Growth and Quranic Engagement

The evening is an ideal time for reading Islamic books, studying tafsir, or reviewing the day's Juz of the Quran. Engaging with the Quran during this peaceful time deepens spiritual awareness and provides guidance for life's challenges.

Maghrib Prayer: A Transition to Night

Maghrib, the sunset prayer, marks the transition from day to night. This prayer is followed by reciting adhkar and engaging in Quran recitation or listening to Islamic lectures, offering spiritual nourishment and preparation for the night.

17.5 Night: Reflection, Worship, and Rest

Isha Prayer: Closing the Day with Devotion

Isha, the final obligatory prayer of the day, provides closure and an opportunity to seek Allah's forgiveness. The Prophet Muhammad (peace and blessings be upon him) encouraged sleeping soon after Isha to rise early for Fajr. For some, this is followed by *Tahajjud,* a voluntary night prayer performed in the stillness of the late hours.

Tahajjud: A Deep Connection with Allah

Tahajjud is a time for intimate supplication and reflection. The Quran praises this act: "And during part of the night, pray Tahajjud as an extra [act] of worship for you; it is expected that your Lord will raise you to a praised station" (Quran,

Al-Isra' 17:79). This serene time allows believers to pour their hearts out to Allah, seeking forgiveness, guidance, and strength.

Reflection and Gratitude Before Sleep

Before resting, engaging in *muhasabah* (self-accountability) helps Muslims assess their actions and intentions. Reciting evening adhkar, such as Ayat al-Kursi (Quran, Al-Baqarah 2:255), provides protection and peace. By ending the day with gratitude, believers strengthen their reliance on Allah and resolve to improve.

17.6 Integrating Quran Recitation and Islamic Learning

A Daily Juz for Spiritual Growth

Reciting a Juz of the Quran daily is a powerful practice that fosters a deep connection with Allah's words. This routine allows Muslims to complete the Quran monthly while reflecting on its meanings. Consistent engagement with the Quran serves as a guide, bringing clarity and solace. Abdullah ibn Amr (may Allah be pleased with him) reported: "The Prophet (peace and blessings be upon him) said: 'Complete the recitation of the Quran in one month.'" (Sahih Bukhari, 5054; Sahih Muslim, 1159).

Dedication to Islamic Knowledge

Setting aside time each day for Islamic learning ensures steady spiritual growth. Whether reading books of Hadith and Tafsir (Quranic commentary), exploring Islamic jurisprudence, or studying the Seerah, the life of the Prophet (peace and blessings be upon him), these efforts strengthen faith and enrich understanding.

17.7 Living a Purposeful Routine in a Modern World

Balancing Faith and Responsibilities

Islam encourages balance between worldly and spiritual pursuits. The Quran states, "But seek, through that which Allah has given you, the home of the Hereafter; and [yet], do not forget your share of the world" (Quran, Al-Qasas

28:77). Muslims are reminded that fulfilling worldly responsibilities, such as work and family obligations, can be acts of worship when aligned with sincere intentions.

Maximizing Time

The Prophet Muhammad (peace and blessings be upon him) said, "Take advantage of five matters before five things: your youth before you become old, your health before you fall sick, your wealth before you become poor, your free time before you become busy, and your life before your death" (Musnad Ahmad, 23413; Sunan Al-Bayhaqi, 5937). Time is a precious resource, and effective management ensures that each day contributes to both worldly success and spiritual growth.

Transforming Routine into Worship

Through intentionality, Muslims can transform mundane tasks into opportunities for worship. Whether completing chores, working with integrity, or helping others, these actions become spiritually meaningful when done for Allah's sake.

17.8 Special Friday Routine

Friday, or *Yawm al-Jumu'ah*, holds a special place in Islam as the most blessed day of the week. It is a time for heightened worship, reflection, and seeking Allah's blessings. Incorporating Quranic recitation, acts of worship, and communal prayers into the Friday routine enhances its spiritual significance.

The Virtues of Friday

Friday is described in the Hadith as the most sacred day of the week. The Prophet Muhammad (peace and blessings be upon him) said:
"The best day on which the sun has risen is Friday; on it, Adam was created, on it, he was made to enter Paradise, and on it, he was expelled from it. And the Last Hour will take place on no day other than Friday" (Sahih Muslim, 854; Sunan Abu Dawood, 1046).

This day offers an unparalleled opportunity for spiritual growth, collective worship, and connecting with the Muslim community.

Morning Routine: Preparing for Friday

- ### Engaging in Dhikr and Supplications

Begin the day with the morning *adhkar*, as discussed in previous chapters, and add specific invocations for Friday. This includes abundant recitation of *salawat*, as the Prophet Muhammad (peace and blessings be upon him) said: "Increase your salawat upon me on the day of Friday and during its night, for your salawat are presented to me" (Sunan Abu Dawud, 1047; Musnad Ahmad, 10729).

- ### Recitation of Surah Al-Kahf (Quran 18):

Surah Al-Kahf is highly recommended on Fridays. The Prophet (peace and blessings be upon him) said: "Whoever recites Surah Al-Kahf on Friday, it will illuminate him with light between the two Fridays" (Sunan Al-Kubra Al-Bayhaqi, 5856; Al-Mustadrak by Al-Hakim, 3392).

Imam al-Haddad encouraged believers to dedicate time in the morning to read Surah Al-Kahf, reflecting on its lessons of steadfastness, reliance on Allah, and the transient nature of this world. Reciting this chapter not only brings light to the believer but also fosters a deeper connection to Allah's guidance.

- ### Engaging in Extra Quranic Recitation

In addition to Surah Al-Kahf, Friday is an excellent time to read other portions of the Quran. Whether it is a Juz as part of one's regular schedule or selected verses for reflection, dedicating time for Quranic recitation aligns the believer's heart with the spiritual importance of the day.

Preparing for the Friday Prayer

- ### Ghusl (Ritual Bath)

Performing *ghusl* is a Sunnah of the Prophet Muhammad (peace and blessings be upon him) on Fridays. He said: "Whoever takes a bath on Friday, cleans himself as much as he can, uses oil or perfume, goes to the mosque and does not force his way between two people, prays as much as is written for him, and remains silent while the Imam is speaking, his sins between that Friday and the next will be forgiven" (Sahih Bukhari, 883).

- ### Wearing Clean and Modest Attire

Dressing in clean, modest clothing is recommended for the Friday prayer, reflecting the sanctity of the occasion. Men are also encouraged to use perfume or *itr* (non-alcoholic fragrance).

- **Arriving Early to the Mosque**

The Prophet Muhammad (peace and blessings be upon him) said: "Whoever takes a bath on Friday and purifies himself as much as he can, then goes early to the mosque, it is as though he sacrificed a camel. The one who comes at the second hour, it is as though he sacrificed a cow. The one who comes at the third hour, it is as though he sacrificed a ram. The one who comes at the fourth hour, it is as though he sacrificed a chicken. The one who comes at the fifth hour, it is as though he sacrificed an egg. When the Imam comes out, the angels close their record books and listen to the sermon." (Sahih al-Bukhari, 881; Sahih Muslim, 850). Arriving early allows for engagement in additional worship, such as voluntary prayers, Quranic recitation, and *dhikr*.

The Friday Prayer: Jumu'ah

The Friday prayer, or *Salat al-Jumu'ah*, is obligatory for adult Muslim men and a recommended act of worship for women. It replaces the Dhuhr prayer on this day, which is performed in the congregation and preceded by a khutbah (sermon).

- **Listening to the Khutbah**

The khutbah is an integral part of the Friday prayer. Attentively listening to the sermon is not only an obligation but also a source of valuable Islamic guidance. The Prophet Muhammad (peace and blessings be upon him) said: 'If you say to your companion on Friday, 'Be quiet,' while the Imam is delivering the sermon, then you have engaged in idle talk" (Sahih Bukhari, 934; Sahih Muslim, 851).

- **The Two Rak'ahs of Jumu'ah**

The prayer consists of two rak'ahs, which are prayed in the congregation after the khutbah. It is a short yet powerful act of worship that fosters unity and collective remembrance of Allah.

Afternoon and Evening Worship

- **Post-Jumu'ah Reflections and Dhikr**

After the Jumu'ah prayer, believers are encouraged to engage in personal reflection and dhikr. Recite *SubhanAllah* (Glory be to Allah), *Alhamdulillah*

(All praise is due to Allah), and *Allahu Akbar* (Allah is Greater) as part of the Sunnah.

- **Continuing Salawat**

Throughout the day, increase *salawat* upon the Prophet Muhammad (peace and blessings be upon him). This act of devotion is a means of attaining Allah's mercy and drawing closer to Him. As the Prophet (peace and blessings be upon him) said: "Whoever sends blessings upon me once, Allah will send blessings upon him tenfold, erase ten sins, and raise him by ten degrees." (Sunan An-Nasa'i, 1297; Jami' at-Tirmidhi, 3476).

- **Voluntary Acts of Worship**

The afternoon offers an opportunity to perform Sunnah or voluntary prayers, read more Quran, or engage in acts of kindness and charity. For example, visiting family or helping someone in need aligns with the spirit of Friday as a day of community and service.

Evening Worship: Concluding Friday with Devotion

- **Recitation of Ayat al-Kursi and The Three Quls**

As the evening approaches, recite Ayat al-Kursi and the Three Quls for protection through the night. These recitations fortify the believer's heart against harm and provide spiritual peace.

- **Du'a at the Hour of Acceptance**

The Prophet Muhammad (peace and blessings be upon him) said: "There is an hour on Friday in which no Muslim makes dua, seeking good from Allah, but it will be granted to him" (Sahih Bukhari, 935; Sahih Muslim, 852). In another narration: "It is a short period of time." (Musnad Ahmad, 7631). This hour is often considered the last hour before Maghrib. Use it to make heartfelt supplications for forgiveness, blessings, and guidance.

- **Maghrib and Isha Prayers**

Conclude the day with the Maghrib and Isha prayers, complementing them with additional Quranic recitations such as Surah Al-Mulk and the last two verses of Surah Al-Baqarah. These recitations bring protection and blessings as the believer transitions into the night.

Friday is a day filled with unique blessings and opportunities for spiritual growth. By incorporating Quranic recitation, such as Surah Al-Kahf, engaging in abundant *salawat*, and attending the Jumu'ah prayer, Muslims can maximize the rewards of this sacred day. With a focus on *dhikr*, *du'a*, and reflection, Friday becomes a weekly spiritual renewal, enriching one's connection with Allah and strengthening faith for the days ahead.

Conclusion

A day in the life of a Muslim is an intricate blend of worship, responsibilities, and self-improvement. By integrating regular Quran recitation, Islamic learning, and mindful routines, Muslims can balance their worldly and spiritual obligations, leading a life of purpose and fulfillment. This comprehensive approach ensures success in both this life and the Hereafter, reminding believers that every moment is an opportunity to grow closer to Allah.

CHAPTER EIGHTEEN

Role of Mosques and Islamic Centers in Nurturing Faith

M osques and Islamic centers have been central to Muslim communities for centuries, serving as places of worship, centers of learning, and hubs of social and spiritual activity. In Islamic history, mosques were more than just spaces for prayer; they were also environments for community building, charitable efforts, and personal development. This chapter explores the historical role of mosques, the importance of successful Islamic centers, the challenges they face, and ways in which they can be strengthened to fulfill their purpose in the modern world.

18.1 The Historical Significance of Mosques

Since the time of the Prophet Muhammad (peace and blessings be upon him), the mosque has been the cornerstone of Muslim life. The first mosque built by the Prophet (peace and blessings be upon him), Masjid Quba, was a place of worship, community, and service. Later, the Prophet (peace and blessings be upon him) established Masjid an-Nabawi (the Prophet's Mosque) in Madinah, which became the model mosque for all future generations. This mosque served multiple roles: it was a place for prayer, a center for learning, and a gathering place where the community could discuss social issues, resolve conflicts, and engage in collective worship.

1. **Mosques as Centers of Worship and Spiritual Growth**:

   ○ Mosques are primarily places where Muslims come to worship Allah. Prayer, recitation of the Quran, and spiritual reflection are the main functions of a mosque, offering believers a sacred space to draw closer to Allah. The Quran highlights the significance of mosques, stating,

"In houses [of worship] which Allah has ordered to be raised, in them His name is remembered" (Quran, An-Nur 24:36). Praying in congregation, particularly the Friday prayer (*Jumu'ah*), not only strengthens one's faith but also builds a sense of unity and solidarity among believers.

○ Mosques also provide spiritual nourishment beyond prayer. They host religious lectures, Quranic classes, and workshops that deepen knowledge and enhance spiritual growth. These programs help individuals connect with Islamic teachings and understand how to implement them in their daily lives. Through these gatherings, the mosque becomes a space of learning, encouraging believers to live with purpose and moral integrity.

2. **Mosques as Centers of Learning**:

○ Historically, mosques were the primary centers of education in the Muslim world. Scholars and students would gather in mosques to study Islamic sciences, such as Quranic exegesis, Hadith, jurisprudence (*fiqh*), and spirituality (*tasawwuf*). Great scholars like Imam Malik, Imam Abu Hanifa, and others taught in mosques, creating a legacy of learning that continues to inspire Muslims today.

○ In addition to religious knowledge, mosques historically played a role in teaching practical skills and knowledge that benefited society. Topics like mathematics, astronomy, and medicine were often discussed within the mosque setting, demonstrating that Islamic education values both spiritual and worldly knowledge. Today, mosques can continue this legacy by offering classes on a range of topics, helping to create well-rounded individuals who contribute positively to their communities.

3. **Mosques as Centers for Social Justice and Charity**:

○ The mosque is a place that reflects the principles of social justice and charity, two key pillars of Islamic ethics. During the Prophet's time, mosques were places where community needs were addressed, and resources were mobilized to support the less fortunate. Masjid an-Nabawi served as a center for social welfare, providing shelter to the homeless, food for the needy, and a gathering place for charitable efforts.

- Mosques today carry on this tradition by organizing charity drives, fundraising for local and global causes, and supporting those in need within the community. These efforts foster a sense of social responsibility and compassion, reminding believers of their duty to care for others and strive for justice in society.

18.2 Contemporary Success Stories: Positive Impacts of Effective Mosques and Islamic Centers

Many mosques and Islamic centers around the world have successfully adapted to meet the needs of their communities, offering programs that go beyond traditional worship. These centers have become vibrant hubs for education, social outreach, and interfaith dialogue, positively impacting both Muslim and non-Muslim communities.

1. **Community Education Programs**:

   - Some Islamic centers have developed comprehensive educational programs that cater to individuals of all ages, from children's Quran classes to adult workshops on Islamic history and contemporary issues. These centers recognize the importance of nurturing faith from a young age, as well as providing ongoing education for adults.

   - For example, the Islamic Center of Southern California has established youth programs, women's study groups, and weekly lectures that engage members of the community in meaningful learning. These programs help individuals develop a strong Islamic identity and provide them with the tools to address modern challenges with a grounded faith.

2. **Youth Engagement Initiatives**:

   - Successful mosques recognize the need to engage young people in a way that resonates with their unique experiences and challenges. Youth programs that include mentorship, social events, and leadership training provide a safe and welcoming space for young Muslims to explore their faith and connect with their community.

   - The East London Mosque in the UK is a notable example of youth-focused programming. The mosque offers a wide range of activities for young people, including sports events, career workshops, and religious study sessions. This inclusive approach helps youth feel a sense of belonging and purpose, while also preparing them to contribute positively to society.

3. Social Services and Support:

- Many Islamic centers have expanded their role to include social services, such as mental health counseling, marital counseling, and support for individuals facing financial hardship. These services address the holistic needs of the community, providing both spiritual and practical support.

- In North America, the Islamic Society of North America (ISNA) has developed a counseling program that addresses the mental health needs of the Muslim community. By offering resources for mental wellness, Islamic centers like ISNA demonstrate that mosques are not just places for worship but are also centers of holistic well-being.

4. Interfaith and Community Outreach:

- Some mosques have excelled in fostering interfaith dialogue and building bridges with other religious communities. These efforts promote mutual understanding, reduce prejudice, and contribute to a sense of unity among people of different faiths.

- The Islamic Cultural Center of New York is a prime example, regularly hosting interfaith events and inviting local leaders from various faith traditions to engage in discussions. This approach promotes peace and harmony, showing that Islamic centers can serve as valuable assets to society by advocating for mutual respect and cooperation.

18.3 Failures and Challenges in Masjid Leadership

Despite the many successes of mosques and Islamic centers, they also face significant challenges that can hinder their ability to fulfill their purpose. Common issues include lack of inclusivity, cultural barriers, financial mismanagement, and ineffective leadership. Addressing these challenges is crucial for creating mosques that truly serve the diverse needs of the Muslim community.

1. **Lack of Inclusivity and Accessibility**:

   ○ Some mosques fail to be inclusive spaces, excluding women, youth, or converts from meaningful participation. In some cases, cultural practices from certain backgrounds are imposed, which can make others feel unwelcome or marginalized.

   ○ Inclusivity is essential for creating a supportive community. Mosques should be accessible to everyone, regardless of gender, ethnicity, or background. Making space for women, for example, by providing suitable prayer areas and involving them in leadership roles, is crucial for fostering a mosque environment that is welcoming and inclusive.

2. **Cultural Barriers**:

   ○ Some mosques are influenced by cultural practices that may alienate members from other backgrounds. For instance, mosques established by immigrant communities sometimes prioritize the language, customs, and traditions of the founders' home countries, which can create a barrier for those unfamiliar with these cultural practices.

   ○ A successful mosque must recognize that Islam is a universal religion and should reflect the diversity of its congregation. Emphasizing Islamic values over cultural customs can help mosques become spaces where people from all backgrounds feel welcomed and valued.

3. **Financial Mismanagement and Resource Limitations**:

   ○ Many mosques struggle with financial sustainability, which can lead to a lack of resources for programming, maintenance, and staff. In some cases, financial mismanagement or lack of transparency can erode trust within the community, leading to reduced support and participation.

   ○ Proper financial management, transparency, and accountability are essential for building trust and ensuring that resources are used effectively. Establishing a clear financial plan and implementing best practices in fundraising can help mosques meet the needs of their communities without compromising on quality or integrity.

4. Leadership Challenges and Lack of Vision:

- ○ Effective leadership is critical for a mosque's success. However, some mosques suffer from a lack of qualified leaders who understand the needs of the community, particularly in non-Muslim-majority countries. In some cases, leaders may lack the vision or skills needed to develop innovative programs that address contemporary challenges.

- ○ Strong leadership requires not only religious knowledge but also an understanding of community dynamics, youth engagement, and modern challenges. Training imams and mosque leaders in these areas can equip them to serve as effective guides and mentors, fostering a thriving community that is responsive to its members' needs.

18.4 Innovations in Community Outreach and Engagement

To address these challenges, some mosques have adopted innovative approaches to better serve their communities. By focusing on inclusivity, intergenerational engagement, and responsive programming, these mosques have become examples of how Islamic centers can adapt to meet the evolving needs of modern society.

1. Incorporating Technology for Greater Reach:

- ○ Some mosques have embraced technology to expand their reach, using online platforms to broadcast sermons, lectures, and events. This approach enables members who may not be able to attend in person to stay connected to the community.

- ○ For example, many mosques began streaming *Jumu'ah* prayers and lectures during the COVID-19 pandemic, allowing individuals to participate remotely. These online platforms continue to benefit the community by providing accessible Islamic content to people worldwide.

2. Creating Safe Spaces for Open Dialogue:

- ○ Some Islamic centers have recognized the importance of creating safe spaces where community members can openly discuss contemporary issues, such as mental health, identity, and family dynamics, from an Islamic perspective. These discussions promote a healthy, well-rounded understanding of Islam and help individuals find guidance and support for personal challenges.

○ For instance, the Muslim Community Center in Chicago hosts regular forums on mental health, identity, and Islamophobia, offering a safe space for open dialogue. This inclusive approach helps build trust within the community and demonstrates that the mosque is a place of compassion and understanding.

3. **Engaging the Broader Society through Outreach**:

• Mosques that actively engage with the broader community, including people of other faiths, play a crucial role in fostering understanding and promoting Islam's message of peace and compassion. Hosting open houses, participating in community service projects, and partnering with local organizations allow Islamic centers to build positive relationships with their neighbors.

18.5 Lessons from Successes and Failures

The successes and challenges of mosques provide valuable lessons for communities seeking to establish purpose-driven Islamic centers. Effective mosques balance tradition with modern needs, creating spaces that are inclusive, responsive, and actively engaged in community well-being. Conversely, challenges such as lack of inclusivity, cultural rigidity, and ineffective leadership highlight the need for openness, adaptability, and a commitment to serving all members of the community.

1. **Prioritizing Inclusivity and Accessibility**:

○ Mosques should be welcoming to all, providing equal access to men, women, and youth. Inclusivity requires intentional planning, such as creating dedicated spaces for different groups and actively involving them in mosque activities and leadership.

2. **Encouraging Community Involvement**:

○ Successful mosques encourage active involvement from community members, allowing them to take ownership and participate in decision-making. This approach fosters a sense of responsibility and pride, empowering individuals to contribute their skills, ideas, and resources.

3. Investing in Youth and Future Generations:

- Engaging youth is essential for the long-term success of a mosque. By offering programs that address the unique challenges faced by young Muslims, mosques can provide a supportive environment where they feel valued and understood. Mentorship programs, youth camps, and leadership training are effective ways to involve young people in the mosque's mission.

4. Transparency, Accountability, and Trust:

- Financial transparency and ethical management are essential for building trust within the community. When mosque leaders uphold these values, they foster a culture of honesty and integrity, encouraging community members to invest in the mosque's mission.

In conclusion, mosques and Islamic centers are crucial in nurturing faith, building community, and promoting social justice. By learning from the successes and failures of mosques, communities can create Islamic centers that reflect the principles of Islam, cater to the diverse needs of the Muslim population, and positively impact the broader society. When mosques fulfill their potential as centers of worship, learning, and community support, they embody the spirit of Islam, becoming beacons of faith, compassion, and unity for generations to come.

CHAPTER NINETEEN

Community Building and Social Responsibility

I slam strongly emphasizes community, encouraging believers to work together to build a society grounded in justice, compassion, and collective responsibility. A community rooted in Islamic principles not only supports individual spiritual growth but also embodies values that contribute to the welfare of society at large. This chapter explores the Islamic principles of community building, the role of social responsibility, successful examples from the Muslim world, challenges to community cohesion, and strategies to foster resilient, inclusive communities.

19.1 Service to Humanity as a Core Purpose in Islam

One of the primary purposes of a Muslim's life is service to humanity. Islam teaches that worship is not limited to rituals alone but extends to helping others, building a supportive community, and working for social justice. The Prophet (peace and blessings be upon him) said, "The best of people are those who bring the most benefit to others." (Al-Mu'jam Al-Awsat by At-Tabarani, 5787). This emphasis on benefiting others is a central theme in Islam and is reflected in various Quranic verses and Prophetic teachings.

    1. **Islamic Ethics of Service**:

        ◦ Serving humanity is deeply rooted in Islamic teachings on compassion, justice, and charity. The Quran frequently calls believers to care for the vulnerable, support the poor, and defend the oppressed. For instance, Allah states, "And they give food in spite of love for it to the needy, the orphan, and the captive, [saying], 'We feed you only for the countenance of Allah. We wish not from you reward or gratitude'" (Quran, Al-Insaan 76:8-9). This verse highlights the selflessness and sincerity that should characterize a Muslim's actions.

○ Islam's emphasis on service goes beyond individual acts of kindness; it includes establishing institutions and systems that ensure fairness and compassion at a societal level. For example, the institution of *zakat* (charitable giving) is designed to support the community's most vulnerable, promoting economic balance and reducing inequality.

2. The Prophet Muhammad's Example in Community Building:

○ The Prophet Muhammad (peace and blessings be upon him) exemplified service to humanity in his actions, teachings, and interactions with others. He established a community in Madinah that was inclusive, supportive, and just, ensuring that every member felt valued and protected. When the Prophet (peace and blessings be upon him) arrived in Madinah, he created bonds of brotherhood between the emigrants (Muhajirun) and the residents (Ansar), fostering a sense of solidarity and mutual support.

○ The Prophet's care extended to people from all backgrounds, including non-Muslims, showing that Islam encourages compassion and respect for all humanity. His leadership in Madinah serves as a model for building communities that uphold the dignity and well-being of each member, regardless of their social or economic status.

3. Social Responsibility as an Integral Part of Worship:

1. Social responsibility in Islam is not a separate endeavor from worship but is an integral part of it. Acts of charity, kindness, and social justice are considered forms of worship when done for Allah's sake. A believer's spirituality is reflected in their interactions with others, as the Prophet (peace and blessings be upon him) said, "None of you [truly] believes until he loves for his brother what he loves for himself." (Sahih Bukhari, 13; Sahih Muslim, 45).

2. This holistic understanding of worship encourages Muslims to actively participate in their communities, contributing to social harmony, well-being, and development. When a community prioritizes social responsibility, it creates an environment where faith is lived and

practiced through compassionate actions and collective support.

19.2 Examples of Successful Islamic Community Initiatives

Various Islamic communities worldwide have successfully implemented initiatives that address their members' social, educational, and economic needs. These programs demonstrate how Islamic principles can be applied to meet contemporary challenges, fostering unity and mutual support.

1. **Educational Programs**:

   ○ Many Islamic organizations have established educational programs that serve the needs of their communities. These programs range from Quranic and Islamic studies classes to tutoring sessions for academic subjects, mentorship programs, and vocational training. The goal is to equip community members with knowledge and skills that empower them to succeed in both spiritual and worldly matters.

   ○ For instance, the Islamic Society of North America (ISNA) provides leadership training, youth programs, and workshops on various topics. These educational initiatives empower individuals with the knowledge and tools to thrive in society while staying grounded in their faith. Such programs are particularly beneficial for young Muslims, who face unique challenges related to identity, peer pressure, and societal expectations.

2. **Health and Well-being Initiatives**:

   • Some Islamic centers and organizations have created health and wellness programs addressing physical and mental health. These programs include workshops on mental health awareness, physical fitness classes, and support groups for individuals facing challenges such as addiction or family issues.

   • For example, in the United Kingdom, the Muslim Youth Helpline offers counseling and support services to young people struggling with mental health issues, addiction, and identity crises. By addressing these needs, Islamic organizations play a vital role in supporting the holistic well-being of their communities, demonstrating that Islam cares for both the spiritual and physical aspects of a person's life.

3. Community Development and Economic Support:
- Economic empowerment is another essential aspect of community building. Many Islamic organizations provide financial support to those in need through *zakat* funds, interest-free loans, and job placement programs. These initiatives help individuals become self-sufficient and contribute positively to society.

- An example of successful economic support is the UK's National Zakat Foundation (NZF), which provides emergency financial aid, housing assistance, and job training to help those in need. Such programs not only alleviate financial hardships but also promote self-reliance and resilience.

4. Interfaith and Community Outreach:
- Some Islamic communities have fostered positive relationships with other faith groups through interfaith initiatives and community outreach programs. These efforts build bridges of understanding and promote harmony within society.

- The Islamic Center of Southern California (ICSC) regularly hosts interfaith events, dialogues, and joint service projects, promoting understanding and cooperation among diverse communities. These initiatives help dispel misconceptions about Islam and showcase the values of compassion, respect, and cooperation that Islam advocates.

19.3 Challenges in Community Development and Social Responsibility

While many Islamic communities have succeeded in their initiatives, they also face several challenges that can hinder effective community building and social responsibility. Understanding these challenges is essential for developing strategies to foster a stronger, more resilient community.

1. **Sectarian Divisions and Lack of Unity**:

    ◦ Sectarianism is one of the most significant challenges facing Muslim communities today. Differences in interpretation, cultural backgrounds, and practices can sometimes lead to division, creating barriers to unity and cooperation.

    ◦ Building a unified community requires focusing on common values and goals rather than differences. Emphasizing the core principles of Islam—such as justice, compassion, and mutual respect—can help unite diverse groups under a shared purpose. Community leaders must actively promote inclusivity, tolerance, and dialogue to overcome divisive tendencies.

2. Generational Gaps:

- Generational differences can also pose a challenge to community building. Older and younger generations may have different views on issues like cultural practices, technology use, and engagement with broader society. These differences can lead to misunderstandings and disconnects within the community.

- Addressing generational gaps requires open communication, respect for each generation's experiences, and a willingness to adapt. Programs that encourage intergenerational dialogue and mentorship can foster mutual understanding, allowing each group to benefit from the other's insights and perspectives. Youth engagement programs, in particular, are essential for making young people feel valued and heard within the community.

3. Financial Constraints and Limited Resources:

- Many Islamic organizations struggle with limited financial resources, which can hinder their ability to provide essential services, maintain facilities, and develop new programs. Financial constraints can also lead to burnout among volunteers and staff, who may lack the resources to carry out their responsibilities effectively.

- To overcome these challenges, communities should establish sustainable funding strategies, including transparent fundraising efforts, zakat collection, and partnerships with local businesses. Proper financial planning and accountability are essential for building trust within the community and ensuring that resources are used effectively.

4. Adapting to Modern Challenges:

- Islamic communities must navigate contemporary challenges such as Islamophobia, media bias, and the influence of secular ideologies. These issues can affect how Muslims perceive their identity, interact with broader society, and engage in community initiatives.

- Addressing these challenges requires a proactive approach that includes media literacy, community education, and interfaith outreach. Islamic centers can offer workshops and resources that empower community members to engage confidently with society while preserving their values. Collaborating with other communities to address common social issues can help counteract stereotypes and foster mutual understanding.

19.4 Building Resilient, Inclusive, and Sustainable Communities

Despite the challenges, Muslim communities around the world are actively working to create resilient, inclusive, and sustainable communities that embody Islamic values. These communities can build a strong foundation for future growth and social impact by prioritizing inclusivity, engaging youth, and promoting transparency and accountability.

1. **Fostering Inclusivity and Unity**:

   ○ Inclusivity is essential for building a cohesive community. Islamic centers should welcome individuals from all backgrounds, including converts, women, youth, and people from diverse ethnic groups. Providing spaces and programs catering to different needs can help make the community feel like a safe and welcoming environment.

   ○ One way to foster inclusivity is by involving different groups in decision-making and leadership roles. Creating a diverse leadership team ensures that various perspectives are represented, allowing for more comprehensive and effective decision-making.

2. **Investing in Youth and Intergenerational Engagement**:

   ○ Youth are the future of any community, and investing in their development is essential for long-term growth. Islamic centers should offer youth programs, mentorship, and leadership training to help young Muslims develop a strong sense of identity and purpose. When youth feel valued, they are more likely to remain engaged in the community and contribute positively.

   ○ Intergenerational engagement also plays a crucial role in community resilience. Programs encouraging mentorship and dialogue between older and younger members foster mutual respect, understanding, and a sense of continuity. By bridging generational gaps, communities can benefit from the insights and experiences of each generation.

3. Promoting Transparency and Accountability:

- Trust is the foundation of a healthy community. Islamic centers must practice transparency and accountability to build trust, particularly in areas like financial management and decision-making. Regularly sharing updates on community projects, finances, and goals helps foster trust and encourages members to support the organization actively.

- Accountability also extends to leadership conduct. Community leaders should embody Islamic values of integrity, humility, and service, setting an example for others. By upholding high ethical standards, leaders can inspire confidence and encourage active participation.

4. Creating Sustainable Social Impact Initiatives:

- For them to be effective, community initiatives must be sustainable and designed to address long-term needs. Islamic centers should develop programs that empower individuals and contribute positively to society, such as job training, financial literacy, and mental health support.

- Partnering with local organizations, government agencies, and other faith communities can amplify the impact of these initiatives. Collaborations allow Islamic centers to pool resources, access expertise, and expand their reach, creating a greater positive impact on the community.

19.5 The Prophet's Example of Community Responsibility

The ultimate community responsibility model is the Prophet Muhammad (peace and blessings be upon him). His leadership in Madinah set a precedent for building inclusive, supportive, and compassionate communities. The Prophet (peace and blessings be upon him) established bonds of brotherhood among the Muhajirun (migrants from Makkah) and the Ansar (residents of Madinah), creating a unified community that was committed to mutual support and shared values.

The Prophet's community in Madinah was also inclusive of non-Muslims, emphasizing respect, justice, and peaceful coexistence. This model highlights that a successful community embraces diversity, promotes social justice, and prioritizes the well-being of all members. Following the Prophet's example, Muslim communities today can strive to be sources of guidance, compassion, and positive influence worldwide.

Conclusion

Community building and social responsibility are integral to the Islamic way of life. Islamic communities can become strong, resilient, and compassionate by serving others, promoting inclusivity, and addressing contemporary challenges. Through these efforts, they fulfill their role as witnesses to the truth, embodying the values of Islam and creating a lasting positive impact on society. In following the principles of justice, compassion, and service, Muslim communities become beacons of light, reflecting the true spirit of Islam and inspiring others toward peace, unity, and well-being.

CHAPTER TWENTY

Conclusion: Living Islam with Purpose in Modern Times

The pursuit of purpose is one of the defining aspects of Islam, guiding Muslims to live meaningful, balanced lives grounded in faith, integrity, and social responsibility. As Muslims navigate the complexities of modern life, the need for a clear, spiritually rooted sense of purpose becomes even more important. This chapter revisits key lessons, offers perspectives on how Muslims today can embody the teachings of Islam with purpose, and emphasizes the ongoing journey of living Islam with intention, resilience, and sincerity.

Summary of Key Lessons

Throughout this book, we have explored various aspects of living Islam with purpose, focusing on how individuals and communities can integrate faith into their daily lives, relationships, and communal roles. The following are some of the core themes and insights that have emerged:

1. **Individual Spirituality and Connection with Allah:**

   - One of the primary purposes of a Muslim's life is to develop a close, intentional connection with Allah. This connection is nurtured through daily acts of worship, sincerity of intention (*niyyah*), and regular reflection. By setting sincere intentions and purifying the heart, believers cultivate a relationship with Allah that enriches every aspect of their lives.

   - Daily practices like prayer, dhikr (remembrance of Allah), and dua (supplication) reinforce this connection, helping Muslims stay grounded in faith despite the challenges and distractions of modern life.

2. The Role of Knowledge in Shaping Purpose:

- Knowledge is fundamental to Islam, as it empowers Muslims to understand their faith, implement its teachings, and make informed decisions. Pursuing knowledge is not just a means of personal development; it is an act of worship that brings believers closer to Allah.

- Islamic teachings encourage the pursuit of both religious and worldly knowledge, allowing Muslims to live purposefully, fulfill their duties with wisdom, and contribute positively to society. Knowledge fosters a deeper appreciation of Islam's timeless values, equipping believers with the tools to navigate complex moral and ethical challenges.

3. Trust in Allah and Embracing His Decree (Tawakkul):

- Trust in Allah, or *tawakkul*, is essential for living with purpose, as it teaches believers to rely on Allah's wisdom and embrace His decree with patience. Whether facing personal trials or professional challenges, tawakkul offers believers a source of strength and peace.

- Trusting in Allah's wisdom does not mean resigning to passivity; rather, it involves making sincere efforts while accepting that Allah's plan is ultimately best. This perspective allows believers to handle setbacks with resilience and gratitude, viewing each difficulty as an opportunity for spiritual growth.

4. Community Building and Social Responsibility:

- Islam's emphasis on community reflects its holistic view of purpose, encompassing personal and communal well-being. By working to support and uplift others, Muslims fulfill a key aspect of their purpose: serving humanity as part of their service to Allah.

- Muslims create a just and compassionate society through charity, kindness, and justice. Community initiatives, educational programs, and social services offered by mosques and Islamic centers are vital for addressing individuals' needs and strengthening the collective fabric of the Muslim community.

5. **The Balance between Spiritual and Communal Obligations**:

   ○ Achieving a balance between one's spirituality and social responsibilities is central to living in Islam. Islam encourages believers to integrate their faith into all areas of life, fulfilling their spiritual and communal roles with dedication.

   ○ By prioritizing personal growth and community well-being, Muslims create harmonious and fulfilling lives. A balanced approach to life, grounded in faith, ensures that they can thrive as individuals while positively impacting those around them.

Living with Purpose in the Modern World: Challenges and Opportunities

The modern world presents unique challenges and opportunities for Muslims seeking to live with purpose. From rapid technological advancements to social and political changes, Muslims today must navigate an environment that can be both supportive and challenging to their faith. By understanding these dynamics, Muslims can develop strategies for staying connected to their purpose, rooted in Islamic values, and equipped to face contemporary issues.

1. **The Challenge of Secularism and Materialism**:

   ○ Secularism and materialism are prevalent in modern society, often promoting a worldview prioritizing personal ambition and material wealth over spiritual fulfillment and social responsibility. This perspective can create tension for Muslims, as it conflicts with the Islamic emphasis on humility, simplicity, and devotion to Allah.

   ○ To counter this challenge, Muslims must remain grounded in their faith and resist the pressure to conform to secular or materialistic values. By embracing a purpose rooted in spirituality, Muslims can lead lives that are fulfilling, meaningful, and aligned with their beliefs, even in a secular world.

1. **Navigating Islamophobia and Misconceptions**:

- Islamophobia and negative stereotypes about Muslims are widespread in certain parts of the world, which can create challenges for Muslims seeking to practice their faith openly. These misconceptions can lead to discrimination, prejudice, and social isolation, making it difficult for Muslims to feel accepted in their communities.

- Despite these challenges, Islam teaches believers to respond with patience, resilience, and dignity. By exemplifying Islamic values of kindness, integrity, and compassion, Muslims can break down stereotypes and promote a positive understanding of Islam. Interfaith dialogue, community outreach, and social engagement are powerful ways for Muslims to build bridges, dispel misconceptions, and contribute positively to society.

2. **Opportunities for Positive Social Impact**:

- The modern world offers unprecedented opportunities for Muslims to positively impact society. Through social media, technology, and global networks, Muslims can connect with others, share Islamic knowledge, and advocate for causes that align with Islamic principles, such as environmental protection, social justice, and humanitarian aid.

- Muslims are encouraged to embrace these opportunities and use their resources for good. By supporting charitable organizations, engaging in community service, and contributing to social change, Muslims fulfill a central part of their purpose, embodying Islam's message of compassion, justice, and kindness.

Incorporating Purpose into Daily Life

One of the most practical aspects of living Islam is incorporating purpose into daily actions, creating a life where every moment reflects one's devotion to Allah and commitment to Islamic values. This intentional approach to life allows Muslims to stay connected to their faith, even in routine tasks and encourages them to view each action as an opportunity to serve Allah.

1. **Setting Daily Intentions**:

    ○ The Prophet Muhammad (peace and blessings be upon him) said, "Actions are judged by intentions, and every person will get what they intended." Muslims transform ordinary activities into acts of worship by setting a sincere intention (niyyah) before each action, whether it's work, study, or even relaxation.

    ○ Setting daily intentions helps believers focus on their purpose, ensuring that their actions align with Allah's guidance. For instance, a person who begins their work with the intention to provide for their family and contribute to society elevates their work to an act of devotion.

2. **Practicing Gratitude and Mindfulness**:
    • Gratitude is a powerful practice that strengthens one's connection with Allah and encourages a positive outlook on life. The Quran repeatedly encourages gratitude, reminding believers that "If you are grateful, I will surely increase you [in favor]" (Quran, Ibrahim 14:7).

    • Practicing mindfulness and gratitude helps Muslims stay grounded, fostering an awareness of Allah's presence and the blessings He has bestowed. Muslims cultivate a sense of purpose that guides them toward righteousness by thanking Allah throughout the day and being mindful of their actions.

3. **Acts of Kindness and Generosity**:
    • Islam encourages small, consistent acts of kindness and charity, which benefit others and contribute to a purposeful life. The Prophet Muhammad (peace and blessings be upon him) said, "Your smile for your brother is charity" (Jami` at-Tirmidhi, 1956; Sunan Ibn Majah, 1335), emphasizing the importance of kindness in everyday interactions.

    • By incorporating kindness, generosity, and empathy into their daily lives, Muslims strengthen their purpose and positively impact those around them. Simple gestures, such as helping a neighbor or offering support to someone in need, are opportunities to serve Allah by serving His creation.

4. **Striving for Self-Improvement**:
    • Islam strongly emphasizes self-improvement, encouraging believers to

seek growth in character, knowledge, and faith constantly. By setting personal goals for spiritual, physical, and mental development, Muslims can work toward becoming better individuals and fulfilling their potential.

- This commitment to self-improvement reflects a purposeful approach to life, motivating Muslims to overcome personal weaknesses, cultivate positive habits, and strive for excellence in all aspects of life.

The Importance of Community Support in Living with Purpose

Community plays a crucial role in helping individuals live with purpose. Islam emphasizes the importance of mutual support, collaboration, and accountability in building a strong, faith-centered community. Muslims create a community where each person can thrive by working together, supporting each other's spiritual growth, and fostering an inclusive environment.

1. **Building Bonds of Brotherhood and Sisterhood**:

   ○ The Prophet Muhammad (peace and blessings be upon him) said, "The believers, in their mutual kindness, compassion, and sympathy, are like one body: when one limb aches, the whole body responds with sleeplessness and fever" (Sahih Bukhari, Hadith 6011; Sahih Muslim, 2586). This hadith highlights the importance of unity, empathy, and mutual care within the Muslim community.

   ○ By fostering close bonds of friendship and support, Muslims help each other navigate life's challenges and stay connected to their faith. Whether through shared prayers, study circles, or acts of service, these relationships strengthen each person's sense of purpose and belonging.

2. **Encouraging Accountability and Personal Growth**:
   - Accountability is essential for spiritual growth, as it encourages individuals to remain consistent in their worship and committed to their goals. Close friends and family members can offer valuable feedback, encouragement, and reminders, helping each other maintain a purposeful life.

   - Islamic teachings encourage believers to choose friends who inspire them to uphold Islamic values and avoid harmful behaviors. A supportive network of friends and mentors reinforces one's purpose and provides guidance in times of difficulty.

3. Providing Resources for Spiritual and Personal Development:
- Islamic centers, mosques, and organizations are vital in supporting the community's spiritual and personal development. Through programs such as religious education, counseling services, and community outreach, these institutions provide valuable resources that help individuals strengthen their faith, develop their skills, and contribute to the community.

- By actively participating in these programs, Muslims can stay connected to their purpose, gain knowledge, and benefit from the collective wisdom and experience of their community.

A Vision for the Future: Living Islam with Purpose

As Muslims look to the future, the goal of living Islam with purpose remains as relevant and important as ever. The following are key areas where Muslims can focus their efforts to create a positive impact, strengthen their communities, and uphold the values of Islam in every aspect of life:

1. **Advocating for Justice and Compassion**:

   - Islam's teachings on justice and compassion provide a strong foundation for social advocacy and community service. By working to address social issues, such as poverty, inequality, and environmental degradation, Muslims can embody the values of Islam and contribute to a more just and compassionate world.

   - Muslims are encouraged to engage in projects that support marginalized communities, promote ethical practices, and create sustainable solutions to global challenges. Through these efforts, they demonstrate that Islam is a faith of action, committed to the betterment of all humanity.

2. **Promoting Peace and Understanding**:
- In a world often marked by conflict and misunderstanding, Muslims have a responsibility to promote peace, respect, and dialogue. Engaging in interfaith dialogue, community outreach, and cultural exchange can help bridge divides, dispel misconceptions, and foster mutual

understanding.

- By exemplifying the principles of mercy, tolerance, and kindness, Muslims can serve as ambassadors of Islam, showing others the beauty and wisdom of Islamic teachings.

3. Embracing Change with Resilience and Faith:
  - As the world changes, Muslims must remain adaptable, resilient, and steadfast in their faith. Embracing change with an open mind and a firm heart allows Muslims to respond positively to new opportunities and challenges while staying true to their purpose.

  - By trusting in Allah's wisdom, relying on their community for support, and continuously striving for self-improvement, Muslims can confidently navigate life's changes, ensuring that they remain connected to their faith and grounded in their purpose.

Conclusion and Call to Action

Living Islam with purpose is a continuous journey that requires dedication, self-reflection, and a commitment to serving Allah and humanity. By embodying the teachings of Islam in every aspect of life, Muslims fulfill their role as stewards of Allah's creation, contributing to the well-being of society and inspiring others to seek a life of meaning and faith.

Each individual has the potential to make a positive impact, strengthen their community, and draw closer to Allah. The path may be challenging, but with sincerity, resilience, and support from one another, Muslims can live lives of purpose, beauty, and fulfillment, reflecting the true spirit of Islam. This journey of purposeful living is an invitation to all Muslims to grow, serve, and leave a lasting legacy of goodness for future generations.

End Book Review Request

Dear Reader,

Thank you for joining me on this journey through ***Living Islam with Purpose***. Your engagement and reflection mean so much, and I hope this book has offered you valuable insights and inspiration to integrate faith, balance, and intention into your daily life and community contributions.

As you carry these insights forward, I warmly invite you to share your experience with others. An honest review—whether on Amazon, Goodreads, or your preferred platform—would be invaluable in helping others discover this message and find encouragement in their own path toward purposeful living. Your feedback is deeply appreciated and can make a difference for readers seeking to live Islam fully and meaningfully in our modern world.

Please click the link or scan the QR code below to submit your review.

https://www.amazon.com/review/review-your-purchases/?asin=B0DNJ9Q CLS

Jazakum Allahu khairan for your support.
Aisha Othman

References

- Al-Ghazali, A. H. M. (2015). The Revival of the Religious Cciences (F. Karim, Trans.). Islamic Book Trust.
  Al-Ghazali's work, Ihya Ulum al-Din, explores various aspects of Islamic spirituality, knowledge, personal accountability, and community obligations, offering insights that are foundational to understanding purposeful living in Islam.

- Al-Haddad, A. A. (2003). The Book of assistance (M. T. J.Winter, Trans.). Fons Vitae.
  This classical text focuses on the importance of an enriched spiritual life, including discussions of intentions, prayer, and community responsibilities. It provides practical advice for nurturing faith.

- Al-Munajjid, M. S. (n.d.). The importance of intentions in Islam. Islam Q&A. Retrieved from https://islamqa.info

- This source provides discussions on the role of intentions(niyyah) in Islam, referencing hadith and scholars' interpretations of the transformative power of sincere intentions.

- Ar-Razi, F. (2009). The great exegesis (Mafatih al-Ghayb)(R. C. Martin, Trans.). Islamic Texts Society.
  Ar-Razi's Quranic exegesis offers insights into verses relevant to community building, social responsibility, and the balance of spiritual and worldly life.

- Sahih al-Bukhari is one of the most authoritative collections of hadith. It provides many of the sayings of the Prophet Muhammad(PBUH) that were referenced throughout the essays, particularly those related to community support, intentions, and spiritual practices.

- Gulen, M. F. (2010). Essentials of the Islamic faith. TughraBooks.

This book covers the essentials of Islamic beliefs, worship, and ethical conduct and how these principles can be applied in modern contexts. It addresses many of the themes of purpose and social responsibility in the essays.

- Hadith of Bukhari.(n.d.). Sahih al-Bukhari. Darussalam.

- Hadith of Muslim.(n.d.). Sahih Muslim (A. Siddiqi, Trans.). Darussalam.

- Ibn Ata'illah al-Iskandari, A. (2009). The book of wisdom (K. Kabbani, Trans.). Islamic Supreme Council of America.
  Kitab al-Hikam by Ibn Ata'illah focuses on spiritual teachings, trust in Allah (tawakkul), and contentment with divine will. It provides valuable perspectives on coping with challenges and trusting Allah's wisdom.

- Khan, M. M., & Al-Hilali, M. T. (Trans.). (1999). Interpretation of the meanings of the Noble Qur'an in the English language. Dar-us-Salam.
  This translation and commentary on the Quran provide a thorough explanation of verses relating to communal obligations, charity, and the ethical framework within Islam.

- Nasr, S. H., Dagli, C. K., Dakake, M. M., Lumbard, J. E. B.,& Rustom, M. (2015). The study Quran: A new translation and commentary. Harper One.
  This annotated translation provides in-depth commentary on Quranic verses, giving context to themes of social justice, community service, and personal purpose.

- Ramadan, T. (2009). In the footsteps of the Prophet: Lessons from the life of Muhammad. Oxford University Press.
  Tariq Ramadan's book explores the Prophet Muhammad's life and teachings on ethics, spirituality, and social responsibility, providing relevant examples of how to live Islam with purpose in the modern world.

- Saeed, A. (2006). Islamic thought: An introduction. Routledge.
  Saeed's book provides an accessible overview of key Islamic teachings, covering topics like spirituality, community obligations,and the balance of worldly and spiritual life.

- Sells, M. A. (1999). Approaching the Qur'an: The early revelation.

White Cloud Press.
This book provides background on early Quranic teachings, highlighting the importance of spirituality, charity, and purpose within Islam's foundational revelations.

- Smith, J. I. (2005). Islam in America. Columbia University Press.
  This book discusses the role of mosques, Islamic centers, and community support networks for Muslims living in non-Muslim-majority societies, providing practical insights into the challenges and successes of community building.

- Sunnah.com (n.d.) Jami' At-Tirmidhi
  https://sunnah.com/tirmidhi

- Sunnah.com (n.d.) Musnad Ahmad
  https://sunnah.com/ahmad

- Sunnah.com (n.d.) Sahih al-Bukhari
  https://sunnah.com/bukhari

- Sunnah.com (n.d.) Sahih Muslim
  https://sunnah.com/muslim

- Sunnah.com (n.d.) Sunan Abi Dawud
  https://sunnah.com/abudawud

- Sunnah.com (n.d.) Sunan An-Nasa'i
  https://sunnah.com/nasai

- The Quranic Arabic Corpus. (n.d.). Word-by-word grammar, syntax, and morphology of the Holy Quran.
  https://corpus.quran.com/wordmorphology.jsp

Made in the USA
Columbia, SC
24 December 2024

48471075R00100